Educational Provision for Children with Autism and Asperger Syndrome

Educational Provision for Children with Autism and Asperger Syndrome

Meeting Their Needs

Glenys Jones

David Fulton Publishers
London

David Fulton Publishers Ltd
The Chiswick Centre, 414 Chiswick High Road, London W4 5TF

www.fultonpublishers.co.uk

British Library Cataloguing in Publication Data
A catalogue record for this book is available from the British Library

ISBN 1–85346–669–7

Typeset by Mark Heslington, Scarborough, North Yorkshire
Printed in Great Britain by The Cromwell Press Ltd, Trowbridge, Wilts.

Contents

To the parents and children I have met in the course of my work, for their strength, optimism, determination and ideas.

Glossary

ASD	Autistic spectrum disorder
DFE	Department for Education
DfES	Department for Education and Skills
DLT	Daily life therapy
EA	Education authority
EBD	Emotional and behavioural difficulty
ESPA	European Services for People with Autism
FE	Further education
HE	Higher education
HFA	High functioning autism
IEP	Individual Education Plan
LEA	Local education authority
LEAP	Life Education of Autistic People
LSA	Learning support assistant
MLD	Moderate learning difficulties
MRC	Medical Research Council
NAS	National Autistic Society
NC	National Curriculum
NLS	National Literacy Strategy
OT	Occupational therapist
PECS	Picture Exchange Communication System
QCAA	Qualifications, Curriculum and Assessment Authority
SALT	Speech and language therapist
SEN	Special Educational Needs
SENCO	Special Educational Needs Coordinator
SLD	Severe learning difficulties
SPD	Semantic pragmatic disorder
SW	Social worker
TEACCH	Treatment and Education of Communication Handicapped CHildren

CHAPTER 1

Autistic spectrum disorders and implications for education

Introduction

During the last 20 years, knowledge and understanding of autism and Asperger syndrome have grown tremendously. Valuable information has been provided by adults with autistic spectrum disorders (ASDs), and professionals now attempt to understand autism from an ASD perspective, rather than solely speculating from the outside on why individuals behave as they do. Those with ASDs are important collaborators in designing provision and services (Peeters, 2000). In writing this book, I have drawn on my experiences from research, from my work as an educational psychologist and from teaching sessions with students, teachers and parents. In addition, time spent with adults with ASDs, particularly with Ros Blackburn and Richard Exley, has influenced my perspective and thinking. My colleague, Rita Jordan, has also provided many valuable insights from her many years of experience within the field of autism.

Elizabeth Newson's work and my discussions with parents have shown the huge importance of taking the parents' knowledge and perspective into account. Conversations with parents have shown that having a child with an ASD significantly affects the lives of families, but often in very positive ways. Parents say that they have acquired skills in living with their child, and in negotiating with professionals and supporting other parents, that they would never have developed otherwise. Many have seen the value of living with a child who brings a different perspective to their lives, whilst acknowledging the very difficult times they have faced as a family. Their energy, skills, determination and love have done much to develop provision and services in the UK. My research and teaching has enabled me to visit many schools to observe and discuss practice. It is heartening to meet staff and professionals who question their work and seek out information and who are committed to making the best provision they can for children with ASDs. Practice in many schools has improved tremendously over recent years and there are many more opportunities for exchanging information and ideas. Guidelines on good practice in ASDs are currently being produced by the Department for Education and Skills (DfES, in press), for policy makers and practitioners, and these should be very useful. There is still much to be done though, in reaching staff in schools who are not yet familiar with the very particular needs of pupils with ASDs and who struggle to teach them effectively. Support for families too is very limited, in many areas, particularly outside of school hours. Parents and siblings are often emotionally and physically exhausted from the constant demands and the harrowing situations they experience, which may be unseen and not voiced, as families have little energy left, or few resources, to convince others that they need support.

Aims and plan of the book

The main aim of this book is to consider educational provision and interventions for pupils with ASDs and the issues which arise when making decisions on these. A consensus is developing on what makes good sense in the education of children with ASDs and the aim is to share knowledge and ideas and pose questions which still need to be explored to enable practitioners and parents to reflect on and enhance their work. It is written for all those working in schools and education authorities, as well as for professionals working in health, social services and voluntary agencies. For all pupils, the main purpose of education is to develop understanding and skills and the ability to apply this knowledge. In the process, it is important that staff develop an effective relationship with, and an understanding of, the particular needs and learning style of each pupil. For pupils with ASDs, this relationship is crucial and needs to be achieved before any effective teaching and learning can occur. On the whole, normally developing children are able to relate effectively to teaching staff and are ready to learn. For pupils with ASDs, though, the relationship is often harder to establish. Given the problems these children experience in understanding communication and social behaviour, teaching staff need to create an environment which is calm and where it is clear what is required. Knowledge and understanding change in the light of research and practice, and ways to define, identify and diagnose ASDs continue to be modified and developed. A brief summary of the current state of knowledge on ASDs is therefore given in this chapter to serve as a background for chapters which follow.

Current understandings of autistic spectrum disorders

Individuals with ASDs differ from each other, reflecting differences in the severity of their autism, their intellectual ability and any additional difficulties. Their personality and experiences, in terms of the response of staff, their family and the wider community will also have an impact. Each pupil needs to be understood and responded to as an individual and caution is needed about making assumptions on the ASD population as a whole. Having said that, it is helpful, initially, to consider the general areas in which a pupil with an ASD differs from other children, to direct staff and parents in assessment and teaching. Common principles are emerging from research and practice which make sense for the majority of pupils with ASDs and which are considered to underpin good practice.

Definitions of autistic spectrum disorders

The term autistic spectrum disorder was suggested by Lorna Wing in 1996 (Wing, 1996a). It is used to describe individuals who have features in common, but who might be quite different from each other. Different subgroups within the spectrum have been described, based on differences noted in behaviour (e.g. Asperger syndrome; high functioning autism; semantic pragmatic disorder (SPD), atypical autism and pervasive developmental disorder – not otherwise specified (PDD-NOS)). All the children in these subgroups share difficulties in three areas to a greater or lesser extent, which are commonly referred to as the triad of impairments (Wing, 1988). The children are affected in:

- their ability to understand and use non-verbal and verbal communication
- their ability to understand social behaviour, which affects their ability to interact with children and adults
- their ability to think and behave flexibly.

There is increasing evidence too, that for some individuals, their sensory perception and responses might be different. Some individuals appear to be over-sensitive and others seem under-sensitive, relative to normally developing children.

Understanding and using non-verbal and verbal communication

Some children with ASDs are delayed in acquiring language, but others develop speech at the usual age. It is estimated that between a third and one half of children do not develop speech (Prizant and Wetherby, 1993) and so need to be taught an alternative means of communication. Other children may develop the ability to speak in complex sentences with an elaborate vocabulary, but may not be able to use this to communicate effectively. Whereas children with other disorders such as severe hearing loss, a specific language disorder or severe learning difficulties will all have communication difficulties, they usually appreciate the purpose of communication and do their best to communicate using gesture, facial expression and other body language. Children with ASDs, however, usually do not understand the purpose of communication and rarely use gesture, facial expression or tone of voice effectively to convey meaning. Individuals with ASDs may find interacting with other people aversive as they do not know how to respond and find others' approaches confusing and anxiety-provoking. They might move away, block out the other person or, in some cases, hit them. Observations of a child's attempts to communicate are often significant in determining whether or not that child has an ASD. All children with ASDs will have difficulty in the pragmatics of language, that is, in the social and functional use of language. They will have semantic difficulties too in understanding the meaning conveyed and the non-verbal elements such as tone, gesture and facial expression.

In summary, in terms of communication and language, a pupil with an ASD:

- may not understand the purpose of communication
- may initiate very little communication with others
- may not show or share an interest with others

- may be delayed in learning to speak or speech may not develop at all
- may make limited or inappropriate use of gesture, eye contact, facial expression and body language
- may have a good vocabulary and speak fluently but not communicate effectively
- may talk at, rather than with, the person
- may have problems in the social timing of conversations.

Social understanding and interaction

The nature of the social difficulties in ASDs is probably the most defining feature and potentially the most disabling. Fundamental difficulties in understanding social behaviour, reading social signals and responding appropriately in social encounters are key characteristics of ASDs. As such, it is important to investigate the child's social behaviour for diagnostic purposes. For individuals with ASDs, of all ages, and at all levels of intellectual ability, their social development is out of line with their general ability. Clearly, many other children with SEN also have problems in relating effectively to others, because of early deprivation, sensory problems or learning difficulties. However, these children generally appreciate that other people have different interests and needs, and learn to understand and read social signals from an early age. They pick up social rules and conventions incidentally, and can adapt these, seemingly effortlessly, in response to the social messages they receive. Individuals with ASDs struggle to understand social behaviour and they comment that other people seem to do things intuitively, whereas they have to work things out consciously and scientifically, which is very effortful (e.g. Grandin, 1995; Gerland, 1997). Those without ASDs are able to process social information whilst performing other tasks. Those with ASDs often need to give their sole attention either to the task or to the social aspect of the encounter. For example, using a calculator outside a social encounter might pose no problems, but operating this successfully when serving a customer might prove very difficult.

The behaviour of normally developing children is increasingly influenced by what their family and peers might think. This is not so for many with ASDs as they are unaware of or have no regard for the social consequences. This can lead to conflict and embarrassment when they do not respect the usual social conventions. Some with ASDs have found a useful analogy is to consider that they have arrived on Earth from another planet and so do not understand Earth rules (Sainsbury, 2000). Accordingly, a website called, *Oops, wrong planet syndrome* has been set up by individuals with ASDs.

In summary, in terms of social understanding and social behaviour, a pupil with an ASD:

- may actively avoid other people
- may show more interest in objects than people
- is less likely to share in the interests of other people
- is less likely to refer to others in play
- may make physical contact with others but on his/her terms
- may find turn-taking difficult
- may fail to read and understand others' feelings and needs.

Thinking and behaving flexibly

Children with ASDs often do not play with toys in a conventional way, and may spin or flap objects or watch moving parts of toys or machinery for long periods, with intense interest and excitement. Their play tends to be isolated or alongside others. They may imitate certain scenes but not share in the imaginative play of others. Some develop a special interest in a topic or hobby and want to spend much time engaged in its pursuit or in conversation about it. This can be very useful for staff and parents, as the interest can become an incentive to engage in activities which the child views as less desirable. It can also develop skills and activities which lead to leisure pursuits or successful employment. Care has to be taken not to be derogatory about these interests, where children are made to feel the activity is not worthwhile or that it is a problem. Obviously, problems can arise if interests are pursued to the exclusion of all else, but the places and time spent on these can be managed by others. The special interest can be a driving force for the individual, encouraging them to get up in the morning and to leave the safe world of their home.

Some individuals with ASDs can show an extreme reaction to a change in a familiar routine. Given their difficulties in understanding what to do in a particular situation, it is not surprising they feel anxious when this is changed. The desire to stick to the familiar may arise out of the need to know what is going to happen. Whereas most children without ASDs can think through the implications of a particular change and generate coping strategies, a child with an ASD has great difficulty in mentally talking through possibilities. A sense of panic can ensue which may result in challenging behaviour. Where possible, staff and parents need to warn the child about the change and tell them what to do within the changed routine.

Some descriptions of the triad suggest that those with ASDs lack imagination, but this is not strictly true (Jordan and Powell, 1995). Some of the activities in which individuals engage and the comments they make are highly creative. Spending time in their company can be inspiring and refreshing as they see and comment on aspects of everyday environments that others have screened out. They do, however, have difficulties in social imagination. They may engage in pretend play but have problems in developing a story with others. In terms of literature, they are likely to prefer factual books and those with a clear story line. Many children with ASDs enjoy watching cartoons on video and repeatedly play back, often clips of certain actions. Some parents have major difficulties in managing their child's video viewing (Nally *et al.*, 2000) and this can be a significant source of stress. Against this, watching videos can be a relaxing leisure activity for some and may be put to educational use. One family successfully created an educational video for their son, Adam (Zihni and Zihni, 1996). They illustrated the meanings and sounds of key words and videoed specific situations where he needed to communicate, using his sister and other family members as models (e.g. going to the toilet at night; accidentally hurting himself). His parents played the same scenes repeatedly to Adam and felt his understanding and communication developed as a result over a two-year period.

In summary, in terms of flexibility of thinking and behaviour, a pupil with an ASD:

- may engage in repetitive activity with or without materials (e.g. twiddling; spinning; flicking)

- may have a special interest which occupies much time and energy
- may play in an unconventional way and have limited pretend play
- may resist changes to familiar routines or plans
- may pursue his/her own agenda and exclude the suggestions of others
- will prefer to be in control and stay in control of what happens.

Sensory perception and responses

Many adults with ASDs report being particularly sensitive to certain sounds, sights, textures and smells (Grandin, 1995; Lawson, 1998). This has implications for the pupil's home and school environment and may explain their response to a change of clothes, new foods, and sights and sounds. Some children appear to be under-sensitive to certain stimuli (Myles *et al.*, 2000a) and some parents have reported their child seems to tolerate high levels of pain. The lack of reaction to pain by some individuals, though, might be to avoid human attention. Whatever the underlying reason, it is important for staff and parents to check a pupil's physical state, on a regular basis, and not to rely on, or assume, that the child will indicate that s/he is in pain.

It is not necessary to set up a distraction-free, picture-free, grey environment for all pupils with ASDs. Some pupils will be able to work in ordinary mainstream classrooms with minor changes to the physical environment (e.g. providing a safe haven). Others will require a classroom that is much less stimulating, where it is very clear what happens in each of the different areas. In a school for children with severe learning difficulties, Jordan *et al.* (1999) describe the classroom for the youngest children which had the curtains drawn, soft lighting and almost bare walls. There was a high shelf with attractive materials out of reach of the children with coloured photographs below, so that the children could point to the photograph to get the toys. As the children became accustomed to the school routines, the classrooms became increasingly like those in the rest of the school. Each pupil will need to be assessed and the classroom modified accordingly.

In summary, in terms of response to sensory stimuli, a pupil with an ASD:

- may be distressed by certain sounds (e.g. hands over ears; move away; cry)
- may be sensitive to touch (stiffen when touched; take off shoes or clothes; roll sleeves up or down)
- may be excited or distracted by visual patterns (e.g. Venetian blinds)
- may resist new foods or experiences (dislike unfamiliar tastes, textures or smells).

Intellectual ability

When Kanner first identified autism, he thought all the children were of at least average intelligence. It is now known that children with ASDs span the range of intelligence from those having severe or profound learning difficulties to those of well above-average ability. This leads to great diversity within the population and it can be hard to detect the ASD in individuals with severe and profound learning difficulties. Similarly, for those of above average intelligence, skills in other areas may mask their difficulties. Individuals with Asperger syndrome or high functioning autism are therefore often diagnosed late. It used to be thought that as many as 75 per cent of those with autism also had learning difficulties (Rutter, 1978), but a recent study suggests that this percentage might be much lower, given that a greater number of more able children with ASDs are now being identified (Baird, 2000).

Age of onset

It is not possible to accurately establish the exact age of onset for a particular child as precise developmental data and video records are not usually available. However, it is generally agreed that the onset for most children is within the first 36 months of life. This is given as one of the diagnostic criteria in both major diagnostic classification systems (*International Statistical Classification of Diseases and Related Health Problems*, Tenth edition (ICD-10) (World Health Organisation, 1992) and the *Diagnostic and Statistical Manual of Mental Disorders,* Fourth Edition – Revised (DSMIV-R) (American Psychiatric Association, 1994)). There appear to be at least three different subgroups in relation to age of onset. Firstly, there are children who appear to have an ASD from birth, where parents report that the baby was unusual from birth onwards. Then there is a second group of children who appear to be developing normally, up to the age of 15 to 24 months, and who then become less socially responsive and may lose the speech they have developed. The reasons for this apparent regression are not yet known, nor whether these children are different in any way from others with ASDs. Finally, there is a third, very much smaller group, whose development is normal but who then show severe regression in many areas. This latter group are often referred to as having childhood disintegrative disorder or Heller's syndrome (Volkmar and Lord, 1998).

Subgroups within the autistic spectrum

Total agreement does not exist, as yet, on the criteria for the various subgroups, so teaching staff and parents are better advised to focus their attention on the literature on ASDs in general, rather than on the features of a subgroup (Wing, 1996a).

Asperger syndrome and high functioning autism

Children in this subgroup were first identified by Hans Asperger in 1944 (Frith, 1989) and subsequently named after him. According to the diagnostic criteria in the two major classification systems, ICD-10 (World Health Organisation, 1992) and DSMIV-R (American Psychiatric Association, 1994), Asperger syndrome applies to those who are of average or above-average intellectual functioning, who have good spoken language and whose language development was not delayed. It is sometimes referred to as a mild form of autism, but this can be misleading as some individuals are severely affected in their ability to function in everyday life. Their high level of skill in certain areas (e.g. speech and academic skills) can lead others to assume that skills in other areas (e.g. self-care skills; independence skills and social understanding) are at a similar level. Expectations from others may then be too high, and when expectations are not met, criticism and blame can follow, reducing self-esteem and causing depression and challenging behaviour.

Although the diagnostic criteria for autism and Asperger syndrome have continually been developed and revised, debate is still going on about the evidence required for a diagnosis of Asperger syndrome. In practice, the diagnosis is sometimes given to individuals outside the official diagnostic criteria. Some children of below-average intellectual ability have been diagnosed as having Asperger syndrome, largely, it seems, on the basis that they attend a mainstream school. In addition, children with delayed and limited language skills have been diagnosed as having Asperger syndrome, as their skills in other areas have been good. The picture is further confused, as some specialists in the field believe there is another able group who do not fit the criteria for Asperger syndrome, who they term high functioning (Schopler, 1998). Some argue that there is no difference between Asperger syndrome and high functioning autism (HFA) (Kugler, 1998; Leekam *et al.*, 2000). Others argue that people with Asperger syndrome are more likely to be clumsy, socially interested and have a special interest, than those with HFA, who are usually delayed in developing speech and language.

Semantic pragmatic disorder

The diagnosis of semantic pragmatic disorder (SPD) is often given where the child has good structural language skills but has difficulties with meaning and in understanding how language is used in social situations. Rapin (1996) argues that children with SPD have difficulties in understanding language, in word-finding, have an unusual choice of words, have limited conversation skills, may speak aloud to no-one in particular, have poor topic maintenance and give unusual responses to questions. They appear to have no difficulties, though, with grammar or speech sounds, in contrast to other children with specific language difficulties. Some argue that children with SPD have better social understanding than other subgroups within the autistic spectrum. All those with ASDs will have semantic and pragmatic difficulties; the question is whether there is a group of children who only have semantic and pragmatic difficulties, with no difficulties in the other two areas of the triad. Most research suggests that children with SPD also have social difficulties and rigid thinking, but in milder and more subtle forms. Bishop (1989a) wrote a useful paper, which attempted to define the boundaries between autism, Asperger syndrome and SPD. She suggests that the differences between the three are more a matter of degree than a sharp divide. Lister Brook and Bowler (1992) and Gagnon *et al.* (1997) also discuss the use of the term SPD and question whether it can be differentiated from high functioning autism. From the point of view of interventions, it is likely to be helpful to use the same strategies with those diagnosed with SPD as for children diagnosed with ASDs.

Atypical autism

This term is used when some, but not all the criteria for autism are met (e.g. where the child meets the criteria in only two of the three areas of the triad; or where age of onset appears to be after the age of 36 months). Clearly, it is important for staff to know in which areas a child with this diagnosis has difficulties in order to plan appropriately.

Pervasive Developmental Disorder – Not Otherwise Specified

This term is more commonly used in America and like atypical autism, is often used when children do not meet all the criteria for autism. It is sometimes used with reference to children with Asperger syndrome, but being told a child has a PDD-NOS would be much less satisfactory and useful to parents and staff (Howlin, 1998a).

Difficulties which might co-exist with autistic spectrum disorders

Learning difficulties

All children with ASDs will experience some difficulties in learning via the traditional methods used in schools. In this section though, the term learning difficulties refers to those who are below average intellectual ability. Getting exact figures on the proportion of those with ASDs who have learning difficulties is problematic. It was thought that they were in the majority, but a recent study suggests that there may be more children with ASDs of average or above-average intellectual ability, than there are below average ability (Baird, 2000). Nevertheless, a significant number of children with ASDs will also be intellectually well below average. It is likely that ASDs are often unrecognised and undiagnosed in children with severe learning difficulties. Hadwin and Hutley (1998) developed a questionnaire to differentiate those with ASDs in this group. They found that pupils with ASDs showed less joint attention, less eye gaze, had less functional and imaginative play and more unusual or restricted motor behaviours than those pupils with severe learning difficulties alone.

Jordan (2001) has written recently about the particular needs of those with ASDs and severe learning difficulties (SLD). Some argue that the usual approaches taken with pupils with SLDs are sufficient and that there is no need to pay particular attention to the ASD. However, Jordan (2001) argues strongly against this position, stating that the needs arising from ASDs demand a specific and different approach. Pupils with SLDs and ASDs are likely to remain dependent on adults for meeting their basic needs related to dressing, washing and feeding and to have major difficulties in developing social and communication skills. As their perception and response to staff will be greatly affected, it is crucial that carers and staff know the pupil also has an ASD. Otherwise, the environment created and demands made are likely to be inappropriate and potentially harmful and distressing.

Motor difficulties

Some pupils with ASDs have motor problems, including dyspraxia, which affect the planning and coordination of movements. A pupil can have difficulties in handwriting, throwing and catching, and balancing and walking, for example. Speech production and chewing might also be affected. Some children will need a detailed assessment by a speech and language therapist, an occupational therapist and/or a physiotherapist to assess their specific needs in these areas. Other pupils with ASDs have extremely good balance and fine motor control, enabling them to do activities which most normally developing children of the same age could not.

Additional diagnoses

Pupils with ASDs can have other disorders too. It is estimated that about one third of children with ASDs have epilepsy, which often develops in late childhood or adolescence (Volkmar and Nelson, 1990). Some pupils might have a dual or multiple diagnoses (e.g. a serious visual impairment (Cass, 1998) or hearing loss, cerebral palsy, or Down's syndrome (Kent *et al.*, 1998)). Gillberg (2000) has estimated that about 10 per cent of children with Down's syndrome have an ASD. There is evidence that some with a dual diagnosis are only diagnosed in terms of their other impairment and that the ASD is often missed. Other conditions associated with ASD are tuberous sclerosis, Fragile-X syndrome and Tourette's syndrome.

Gender and ethnicity

Four or five times as many males as females have autism in the group with learning difficulties (Lord and Schopler, 1987) and it is thought there may be ten times as many males as females in the high ability group. Wing (1981) has suggested that perhaps males are more susceptible to ASDs. In females, ASDs might be harder to detect, as they may have greater social empathy than males and diagnostic tools may need to be modified accordingly (Medical Research Council, 2001). Children from all cultures and social groups have been diagnosed, but further work needs to be done to evaluate ethnic differences and to improve awareness within ethnic minorities, as they are under-represented in referrals for diagnosis and attendance at support groups and workshops.

Causation

A recent report by the Medical Research Council (MRC), which reviewed the available evidence on causation, stated that there is now 'overwhelming evidence for a biological basis and a strong genetic component. Most researchers believe that ASDs have a variety of causes perhaps all affecting the same brain systems' (MRC, 2001, p. 21). It is thought that there are several genes which act together with environmental factors to cause ASDs, but it is not yet known which these are (Rutter, 1996; Bolton *et al.*, 1994; Bailey *et al.*, 1996; LeCouteur *et al.*, 1996). There are several environmental triggers being studied, although none, as yet, has been scientifically validated. These include illness during pregnancy, childhood illness, food intolerance, and reactions to vaccination and pollutants. It is often difficult to separate out real causes from events such as illness, injury or vaccination, which occur coincidentally at the time the child's difficulties become most apparent. Many children experience problems during birth, have a serious illness or other trauma, but do not develop an ASD, so there are clearly other factors involved.

Psychological theories

There are a number of psychological theories which attempt to explain the behaviours seen in ASDs and how individuals with ASDs perceive, process and understand the world. Three recent theories focus on theory of mind, executive functioning and central coherence. Those working on *theory of mind* propose that individuals with ASDs lack the ability to read and interpret others' emotional and mental states, which may explain the social and communication difficulties seen (Baron-Cohen, 2000). Mind-reading generally develops naturally and is not something which is taught to children. It develops through sharing attention and common interests, and engaging in pretend play. At the age of about four years, children start to lie when they see the potential in making someone else think that something is true when it is not. Children with ASDs tend not to lie and have problems in understanding that someone else is lying to them. This makes them particularly vulnerable. More able individuals with ASDs can eventually work out how others think, but it takes a great deal of effort.

Some psychologists argue that those with ASDs have difficulties in *executive functioning*, that is, in planning and monitoring actions, in inhibiting behaviours and in shifting attention (Ozonoff, 1995; Russell, 1997). They also have problems in generating ideas and adapting responses to suit different situations. The third theory suggests that individuals have *weak central coherence*, so they focus more on details and have problems in integrating the components to obtain the whole picture (e.g. when riding a bike; scanning a picture; understanding the gist of a story) (Happe, 1999). Those with ASDs often have very good visual memories for unrelated strings of information and complex patterns. Differences in central coherence might explain the development of special interests and high levels of skill in particular areas.

In terms of the educational implications of these theories, some materials have been developed for teaching theory of mind (Howlin *et al.*, 1998). However, although some children can successfully be taught the skills to pass theory of mind tasks, these may not generalise and the children's social competence in everyday encounters may not be influenced by such teaching. It is probably more effective to teach children these skills as and when they are engaged in 'everyday' interactions, using such strategies as social commentaries, Social Stories and Circles of Friends, for example (see Chapters 4 and 6). The difficulties children have in planning, sequencing and shifting attention need to be taken into account. Adults need to give children sufficient time to respond and complete tasks and to provide visual cues for the different stages involved. Implications arising from the weak central coherence theory are that time needs to be given to explain and describe the bigger picture, to ensure that the child has understood the other meanings conveyed within a story, a situation or a task.

Prevalence studies

Problems in establishing prevalence

Accurate figures do not exist on the actual number of children and adults with ASDs living in an authority, or in the UK as a whole. It is often implied that it would be a relatively straightforward exercise to obtain such figures. However, this is not easy. The definitions and diagnostic criteria for ASDs are qualitative and largely dependent on observation and the skills and knowledge of those the child meets. There is no medical, biochemical or psychological test for ASDs and so there is a possibility for under- and over-identification. Prevalence figures depend on the assessment tools and methods used, and variations between studies will reflect methodological differences. For a single agency or professional group to have data on all individuals with ASDs is currently not possible. Employing a person or team within a geographical area to identify and collect these data is also problematic. Even if it was possible to locate every individual diagnosed, there are problems in accepting the accuracy of the diagnosis.

Epidemiological studies have often started by asking professionals to identify which children have a definite diagnosis and which children have a possible diagnosis of an ASD, and have then done further checks themselves. But this approach does not pick up children whom professionals do not put forward. Some surveys have therefore decided to look at every member of a specific population (e.g. every child attending a particular school) and used a screening instrument to identify those who might have an ASD and then done more detailed assessment. There are ethical issues to be considered though, if a research team discovers there is a child with an ASD who has not previously been identified.

Surveys in England and Wales (Jones and Newson, 1992b) and in Scotland (Jordan and Jones, 1996) have shown that the actual number of pupils with autism or Asperger syndrome known to education authorities often falls far short of the expected figures. Education authorities rarely keep a separate record of the numbers diagnosed and so the staff of individual schools need to be consulted. Their data are unreliable because there might be no record of the diagnosis on the child's reports; the respondent may not have sufficient knowledge of autism or of the pupils on roll; some respondents are reluctant to use diagnostic labels; and time constraints often prevent the survey forms being completed adequately. It would be useful for education, social services and health authorities to maintain a shared record of those individuals who are identified, so that accurate data are available for planning purposes.

Increase in the numbers of children diagnosed with autistic spectrum disorders

As our knowledge, understanding and awareness increase, more children with ASDs are being identified. Prevalence studies for classical autism give figures of 4–5 per 10,000, rising to 22 per 10,000 for the group with autism and learning difficulties (Wing and Gould, 1979). A study in mainstream schools in Gothenburg, on the prevalence of Asperger syndrome, suggested a much higher prevalence for this group, of 36 per 10,000 (Ehlers and Gillberg, 1993), giving a rate of almost 4 in 1,000. However, this study included children who were delayed in acquiring language, which is outside the usual diagnostic criteria for Asperger syndrome.

A recent report produced by the Medical Research Council (MRC, 2001), which based their figures on two recent reviews of prevalence conducted by Fombonne (1999) and Wing (2001), suggests that there is now fairly good agreement that ASDs affect approximately 60 per 10,000 children under the age of eight and that more narrowly defined autism is found in 10–30 per 10,000. The rate for the whole population is likely to be higher, as many older children are missed and not diagnosed until late childhood, adolescence or adulthood. Taking the 60 per 10,000 figure, this would mean that within a mainstream secondary school with 500 pupils, one would expect to find about three pupils with an ASD on roll, and in an education authority with 50,000 children, there would be at least 300 pupils in total with an ASD. Not all these pupils will have educational needs that require additional support, but many will, so this is a sizeable number for which an education authority has to provide.

There are some professionals who believe that a greater percentage of children are developing ASDs. It is difficult to know whether the apparent increase in numbers is real or due to the increase in awareness and the ability of professionals to diagnose (see Gillberg *et al.*, 1991). Surveys show that the numbers identified usually only reach a rate of 10 per 10,000 or less (Jordan and Jones, 1996; Howlin and Moore, 1997). Wing (1996b) believes that the higher prevalence rates are a result of the increased diagnosis of children with severe learning difficulties and those who are high functioning or with Asperger syndrome. But, a growth in the numbers of young children has been recorded in services where good diagnostic systems have been in place for many years (MRC, 2001). Environmental factors, such as the increased use of pesticides and other pollutants, are being studied as possible triggers. Further research is required to clarify the position. The recent MRC report (2001) concludes that:

> Methodological differences between studies, changes in diagnostic practice and public and professional awareness are likely causes of apparent increases in prevalence. Whether these factors are sufficient to account for increased numbers of identified individuals, or whether there has been a rise in actual numbers affected, is as yet unclear . . .
> (p. 3)

Outcome

As children with ASDs grow older, their understanding and skills increase, and for some, their ASD becomes harder to detect. Outcome studies have shown that intellectual ability, language development, the severity of the original symptoms and the quality of their educational experience are the main determinants of future outcome (DeMyer *et al.*, 1973; Freeman *et al.*, 1991). Expressive language level is probably the strongest indicator of outcome (Schreibman, 1988; Venter *et al.*, 1992) and prognosis seems more favourable for those who initiate social interaction (Koegel, 2000). There have been claims of recovery from autism (Kaufman, 1976; Perry *et al.*, 1995), but the majority view is that ASDs are lifelong.

Over recent years, educational interventions and services have been developed and enhanced. The depressing outcomes reported in earlier texts on autism are no longer valid. In these accounts, the impression was given that it was not possible for those with autism to make significant progress. But these accounts were often based on inadequate provision and on individuals with the greatest difficulties, who were then the main group being diagnosed. Although there is still much to do in terms of creating effective provision for all children with ASDs, and for supporting adults with ASDs; overall, those diagnosed with an ASD receive much more appropriate provision than they did 10 or 20 years ago. In addition, individuals who are more able or with less severe autism are being identified and diagnosed. Some individuals with ASDs (an unknown number of whom are not diagnosed) have always lived independently, been in employment and may have had a partner and children. The proportion of individuals in this group is likely to increase as provision becomes more effective. These adults are able to lead independent, successful lives and may not gain from being told they have an ASD. Others say that knowing their diagnosis has helped them to make sense of themselves (e.g. Gerland, 1997; Sainsbury, 2000).

Optimism

Finally, it is important to foster and maintain a positive and optimistic approach. The success of those with ASDs should be publicised and disseminated to show that, given appropriate support and resources, the difficulties arising from ASDs can be managed effectively and particular interests and skills maximised and valued. It is frequently the response of others that creates the greatest problems for the individual and the family. Increasing awareness of ASDs and changing these responses are likely to enhance the lives of people with ASDs. Adopting perspectives which promote optimism and inclusion, and a belief that teaching staff and parents can make a difference, is essential. Three examples of such perspectives follow. The first is taken from Carol Gray (Gray, 2000) who provides both optimism and a way forward. She maintains that 'we hold more than half the solution' and argues that it is misleading and unfair to refer to a person with an ASD as having a social or communication impairment. This implies that the problem and the solution rests solely with the individual, when in fact, staff, parents, siblings and classmates can alter their language and style of interaction, the demands they make and the environment they create to suit the person's understanding and skills. Taking this view is very enabling, as it illustrates there is much that others can do to improve the daily lives of those with ASDs.

The second example draws from the comments of individuals with ASDs themselves (e.g. Grandin, 1995; Williams, 1996; Gerland, 1997). It is clear they have a different experience of the world and particular skills and interests which provide fresh insights, some of which lead to valuable discoveries and careers. In working in schools and colleges, these can and should be valued, rather than trying to change the individual to behave and respond like others.

The third perspective is to view the difficulties in learning that result from ASDs as differences, since, as for other conditions, they only become difficulties if they are not accommodated (Jordan and Jones, 1999a). Jordan (2001) points out that, as in other areas of disability, autism is no longer viewed as a pathological state but as 'a feature of normal biological variation which may have evolutionary advantages as well as disadvantages and where problems arising from the condition are seen as the result of social attitudes rather than actual disabilities' (p. 6).

Teaching children with ASDs can be challenging and rewarding, but can also lead to feelings of failure, as even experienced staff do not always have a solution to the problems which arise (Hesmondhalgh and Breakey, 2001). Jordan (2001) has said that one needs to be a good detective when working and living with a child with an ASD, collecting evidence from the child's reactions and from the available literature, to determine the response which is likely to lead to success. The chapters which follow aim to help professionals and parents create an effective educational environment in which the pupil can feel valued and safe, and within which s/he can succeed and progress to enjoy a good quality of life as an adult.

Summary

- There is great diversity between pupils with ASDs.
- The criteria for different subgroups is still under discussion.
- It is important to adopt the perspective of the pupil with the ASD.
- More children are being diagnosed with ASDs at an early age.
- More able children are being identified, although their diagnosis is often delayed.
- There is strong evidence for a genetic component in the causation of ASD.
- Establishing prevalence is not easy as there is no conclusive test.
- The current estimated prevalence rate for ASDs is 60/10,000 for children under the age of eight years, but the actual number identified often falls far short of this.
- Taking an optimistic view of a pupil's potential and taking responsibility for altering the environment are likely to be effective strategies in teaching a pupil with an ASD.

CHAPTER 2

Identification and diagnosis

Introduction

This chapter focuses on the identification and diagnosis of autistic spectrum disorders (ASDs). Although teaching staff do not make the diagnosis *per se*, they have much to contribute to the diagnostic process and issues relating to diagnosis often arise in the course of their work. The teacher may be the first professional to raise concerns about a child or may have questions relating to diagnostic reports written by others. Given the potential benefits of diagnosis, in helping staff and parents to make sense of the child, giving access to useful literature and support, the earlier the diagnosis is given, the better. As many children are not diagnosed until they are of school age (Jordan and Jones, 1996; Howlin and Moore, 1997), it is important to raise awareness of staff within mainstream and special schools. Staff then need to know the procedures in their area, for referring a pupil for a diagnostic assessment.

The diagnostic process

The ability of professionals to recognise and identify children with ASDs has improved tremendously in the last few years, to the extent that there has been a significant increase in the numbers of children diagnosed and the age at diagnosis has decreased (Howlin and Moore, 1997). Instruments to screen for and diagnose ASDs continue to be developed. Despite the existence of published diagnostic criteria, however, diagnostic practice varies throughout the UK in terms of the methods used, the professionals involved, the terminology used and the proportion diagnosed. This can be confusing and frustrating for parents and professionals alike. Some children with ASDs are not diagnosed early and some may never receive a diagnosis or are not diagnosed until they are in secondary school or in adulthood. In some areas, multi-agency working parties have been set up to discuss and enhance their practice.

Diagnosis of ASDs can be difficult as there is no medical, biochemical or psychological test and there is much diversity within the population. The presentation of the triad of impairments (as described in Chapter 1) differs from one individual to another and there is a wide ability range within the population. Diagnosis is based on systematic observation and detailed reports on the child's early development. Other childhood disorders or experiences can affect communication, language development and the social behaviour of the child and so professionals need to differentiate ASDs from other disorders. Additional difficulties might co-exist with ASDs which can further complicate the diagnosis.

People involved in diagnosis

The type of professionals involved in diagnosis varies from one area to another, depending on how services have developed and whether individuals have a particular interest or expertise. In practice, a diagnosis of an ASD might be given by a paediatrician, a psychiatrist, a speech and language therapist, a clinical or educational psychologist, or a GP. Others who see the child and family regularly, such as preschool staff, may already have suspected the child had an ASD and referred the child for further assessment. Increasingly, diagnosis is given after a multi-disciplinary assessment, where paediatricians, speech and language therapists, teachers and educational or clinical psychologists offer their views on the same child. In some authorities, there are named educational psychologists or speech and language therapists, who have a specialism in ASDs, who might diagnose a child independently of others. In other areas, medical professionals, such as psychiatrists, paediatricians or community health personnel will make most of the diagnoses. Each geographical area will have its own system with which teaching staff and parents have to become familiar.

As there is no conclusive diagnostic test, professionals can disagree with each other on the diagnosis given to a particular child, which can add to the parents' distress. The recent Department of Health White Paper on learning disability, *Valuing people* (DoH, 2001), comments on the lack of skilled expertise in diagnosing ASDs. A national working party – the National Initiative for Autism: Screening and Assessment (NIASA) – has recently been set up to develop guidelines and protocols for early diagnosis and intervention for preschool and school-aged children.

Screening for autistic spectrum disorders

In an attempt to identify ASDs as early as possible, a number of screening instruments have been developed. The most well known of these in the UK is the Checklist for Autism in Toddlers (CHAT) (Baron-Cohen *et al.*, 1992). Another instrument, developed in America is the Childhood Autism Rating Scale (CARS) (Schopler *et al.*, 1988). A third screening instrument, known as the Childhood Asperger Syndrome Test (CAST) (Scott *et al.*, 2002), has been developed recently to screen for children with Asperger syndrome.

Checklist for Autism in Toddlers (CHAT) (Baron-Cohen et al., 1992)

This screening instrument can be used by GPs or health visitors during a child's developmental assessment at 18 and 42 months. It comprises nine questions for parents and five situations set up to observe the child's response. Information is obtained on sharing attention, pretend play and communication. If a child is not sharing attention, not pointing and not pretending, it may be that the child has an ASD. The CHAT, in itself, does not show definitively that this is the case. Instead, it alerts professionals to children who might have an ASD. Further assessment is needed on children who fail particular items. The CHAT is used in some health authorities, but further work is required on the checklist as it appears to miss children who are high functioning or who have Asperger syndrome. Recent research suggests the CHAT may only identify a third of children with ASDs and may mistakenly identify 2 per cent of children who have not (Medical Research Council, 2001).

Childhood Autism Rating Scale (CARS) (Schopler et al., 1988)

The CARS was developed in America and has 15 areas with items within each, for parents or carers to rate the behaviour and responses of the children, relative to normally developing children of the same age. It can be used to identify children with autism from the age of 24 months onwards. The CARS is limited as a diagnostic tool as it lacks detail and does not provide evidence on early development.

Methods of diagnosis

To make a diagnosis, systematic observations of the child at home and/or in other situations are required, together with a good account of the child's early history from the pregnancy and to the present. The majority of children develop the condition within the first 36 months of life, although there are one or two reported cases of children developing an ASD after this age, as a result of viral encephalitis, for example (Gillberg and Steffenburg, 1987). Other investigations are often made to check whether the child has any additional disorders (e.g. epilepsy; learning difficulties; hearing or visual problems). A number of diagnostic instruments have been developed based on interviews, structured observations and ratings. These often provide a measure of the degree of impairment as well as whether the individual meets the criteria for diagnosis.

Diagnostic instruments need to be used in combination with observations of the child in natural settings and past reports. Very young children, or those with severe learning difficulties, may have a limited range of social and communicative behaviours which makes it difficult to know whether the impairments which characterise ASDs are present. Extended observation and assessment of these children is often necessary. Some practitioners have developed diagnostic assessment procedures based on structured play situations (e.g. Newson, 1993). Cumine et al. (2000) give suggestions as to the type of behaviours and skills to look for in the early years, grouped under the headings of social interaction, communication, play and flexible behaviour. Such data can be gathered by teaching staff over time and this can be of great value in the diagnostic process. Several diagnostic instruments have been developed to aid diagnosis (see Table 2.1). All require training in their use and some are restricted to particular professional groups. Some are based

Table 2.1   Diagnostic instruments for autistic spectrum disorders

Instrument	Target group	Main methods
ADI-R (Lord et al., 1994)	36 months to adult	Semi-structured interview with parents (90 mins)
ADOS (Lord et al., 1989)	6 to 18 years	Observation of 8 semi-structured play situations
PL-ADOS (DiLavore et al., 1995)	2 to 5 years	Observation of 12 play activities (30 mins)
ADOS-G (Lord et al., 2000)	Preschool to adulthood	Observation of semi-structured activities (30 mins)
DISCO (Wing, 2002)	Preschool to adulthood	Semi-structured interview with parents
ASDS (Myles et al., 2000b)	Child to adulthood Asperger syndrome/HFA	50-item checklist completed by parents or staff
ASDI Gillberg et al., 2001)	Child to adulthood Asperger syndrome/HFA	Structured interview
Play-based assessment (Newson, 1993)	Preschool to secondary	Structured observations of play and interview with parents

Key:
ADI-R	Autism Diagnostic Interview – Revised
ADOS	Autism Diagnostic Observation Schedule
PL-ADOS	Prelinguistic Autism Diagnostic Observation
ADOS-G	Autism Diagnostic Observation Schedule – Generic
DISCO	Diagnostic Interview for Social and Communication Disorders
ASDS	Asperger Syndrome Diagnostic Scale
ASDI	Asperger Syndrome Diagnostic Interview

purely on interviews with the parents or carers, whilst others involve observing the child in play situations specifically set up for the diagnostic assessment.

Other sources of information for diagnostic assessment

In addition to structured interviews and observations, there are a number of other sources of data which can be used. These sources are important as they provide a longitudinal perspective and information about the child in the natural settings of home and school. They include:

- past reports on the child
- information from parents and other family members
- observations of the child in different situations at home and at school
- discussions with professionals who know the child well

- direct work with the child
- formal testing
- discussion with the child, where appropriate
- analysis of samples of the child's work and approach to tasks.

Past reports on the child

As ASDs usually develop within the first 36 months, it is important to look for evidence of the triad of impairments during this time. Past reports can be a useful source for older children and adolescents, and can provide data on whether development appears to have been delayed or different in early childhood. As the format and content of reports is likely to differ, it is helpful to transfer data under a series of eight headings which are of particular interest in ASDs, as follows:

- language and communication
- social understanding
- flexibility
- sensory issues
- challenging behaviour
- areas of ability
- special interests or skills
- other areas of difficulty.

Information from parents and other family members

Parents usually realise that something is different about their child from an early age because of the child's lack of response, unusual interaction with others, delay in developing spoken language or their strange play and interests. Osterling and Dawson (1994) analysed home videotapes of the first birthday of a group of 11 children with autism and a group of 11 children who were developing normally. There were already clear differences between the two groups, particularly in the amount of looking at others, but also in showing, pointing and turning to their name. Parents may be reassured by friends and relatives and told not to worry, as children develop at different rates, particularly if the child seems unusually skilled in some areas (e.g. in doing jigsaw puzzles, reading words, naming objects). Similarly, when parents first voice their concern to a professional (whose knowledge and experience might be limited), the child's ASD might not be identified or the difficulties or delay might be attributed to something else (e.g. deafness; prematurity; being a twin) or to problems within the family. One parent, for example, was told her son's behaviour was due to her depression. Although she was prepared to accept this might have an impact, she felt he had more severe and complex problems which could not be explained solely by her own emotional state. She said, 'I was tempted to believe this explanation as it seemed preferable to take this view of his problems, as there was then a chance of rescue and recovery'. He was diagnosed as having Asperger syndrome several years later.

This parent was understandably angry for the years she had felt blamed by teachers and others for her son's anti-social and difficult behaviour.

Observations of the child in different situations at home and at school

Some of the standardised methods given in Table 2.1 (e.g. ADOS and PL-ADOS) include observations of the child in specific situations. The child can also be observed informally in the natural settings of home, preschool group or school. Before observing the child, it is important to consider the type of information required and which situations lend themselves to this. Observing a child on his/her own will provide limited information, as many of the difficulties in ASDs relate to the child's interactions with others. Having predetermined coding sheets on which to record particular behaviours can be useful or long-hand notes can be made and categorised later. Video records can be taken of children to analyse their contact with others, their response to communication, their cognitive and social levels of play, any repetitive behaviours and their ability to follow another person's suggestions. Video recording allows repeated viewings to check on skills and enables others to observe the same situations, which is useful as a reliability check. These records can also serve as a baseline against which future progress can be measured.

Discussions with professionals who know the child well

Information from people who already know the child well is very important, as they are able to give a longer term and broader view of the child than practitioners who are meeting the child for the first time for diagnosis. They are also likely to be the people who continue working with the child and the family in the future. Reports can be requested from these key people or they can be invited to attend part of the diagnostic process. If they are not included in the process, they are likely to feel their opinion is not valued.

Direct work with the child

The degree of direction given to the child during a diagnostic assessment will vary from centre to centre. Some practitioners have a set plan, where they work through a series of play or work tasks, each of which generates particular data. Others might observe the child playing with their parents or keyworkers and take notes on what happens informally. Yet others might use standardised IQ or language tests. Advantages of having a predetermined schedule or test is that data are guaranteed on the required areas of development. A disadvantage is that the novelty of the situation might change the child's usual performance. The more informal approach with familiar adults might generate information on their usual behaviour but run the risk of missing out on information on behaviours which are not generated during the session. A combination of the two methods is likely to yield the most useful information.

Formal testing

Many have written on the issues which arise when using formal tests with children with ASDs (e.g. Baker, 1983; Parks, 1983; Koegel *et al.*, 1997). The majority of tests have not been designed specifically for them. The very nature of ASDs and the problems which arise in understanding other people, particularly on verbal tasks, sensory overload and the ability to switch and focus attention, means that a child may fail on a sub-test, not because s/he lacks the ability being measured, but as a result of other factors. Altering the conditions for administering tests has been found to improve the scores of children with ASDs (Koegel *et al.*, 1997) and practitioners need to be cautious when interpreting the scores of such tests. It is important that test results are not used in isolation but as one of several sources of assessment information in the diagnostic process.

Discussion with the child, where appropriate

For children with good expressive language skills, evidence of their understanding and perspective can be obtained from conversations or from their written work. Existing samples of work might be analysed. Where the child is not able to express his/her views, it is important that those who know the child very well are consulted.

Action which might be taken when staff suspect that a child has an autistic spectrum disorder

Teaching staff might believe that a child has an ASD but no diagnosis has been made. They can collect evidence on the areas in the triad and then discuss this with other staff who know the child and also with staff who have knowledge of ASDs. The next step would be to discuss the information informally with professionals who visit the school (e.g. speech and language therapist, educational psychologist, school doctor). If there seem to be sufficient grounds for a diagnostic assessment, then the evidence needs to be discussed with the child's parents and a referral made to the educational psychology service, community paediatrician or via the family GP.

Potential benefits of a diagnosis

Having a diagnosis has the potential to help in a number of ways. It gives access to relevant literature, to other parents and professionals and to useful forms of support such as outreach teams, training events and parent support groups. Knowing the underlying reasons for the child's behaviour is important in devising strategies to help the child, rather than merely reacting to and speculating on the causes of a behaviour as it occurs. A mother who received the diagnosis when her son was aged four said:

> I felt empowered. In retrospect, the diagnosis marked the beginning of my acceptance of Joseph's problems. I perceived our relationship to be a close one; however, I lacked

the knowledge and understanding of his perception of the world. The diagnosis guided me to the sources of information and services to enable me to help my son. (O'Connell, 1999, p. 14)

Age at diagnosis

It is now possible for experienced practitioners to recognise and diagnose an ASD in many children by the age of 18 months (Baron-Cohen *et al.*, 1992), but in practice, the diagnosis is rarely made until after the age of 36 months. Howlin and Moore (1997) reported that 93 per cent of parents had had concerns about their child's development before their third birthday, but the majority were not diagnosed until well beyond this time. As expertise and awareness increase, the age at diagnosis is decreasing. The study by Howlin and Moore (1997) found the average age for the diagnosis of autism was 5.5 years and for Asperger syndrome 11.3 years. Typically, children with Asperger syndrome are identified when they meet a new social challenge (e.g. playgroup; reception class; secondary school; college; university). Many children with Asperger syndrome or in the high functioning group are not identified until adulthood (Aston, 2000; Sainsbury, 2000) and there are some who are never diagnosed. Individuals in all these groups have often been incorrectly labelled as lazy, defiant, emotionally disturbed, odd and eccentric or wrongly diagnosed with a psychiatric or mental health disorder, such as schizophrenia or obsessive-compulsive disorder. Clare Sainsbury, who was not diagnosed with Asperger syndrome until she was 20 years old, said:

When I didn't have an official diagnostic label, my teachers unofficially labelled me as emotionally disturbed, rude and so on . . . and my classmates . . . labelled me as weirdo, freak and nerd. Frankly I prefer the official label. (Sainsbury, 2000, p. 31)

This serves as a powerful argument for the use of diagnostic labels in ASDs.

Multi-agency approach to diagnosis

As ASDs affect many aspects of the child's life, it is helpful to have different disciplines involved in the diagnostic process. Psychologists in a diagnostic team can give information on the child's intellectual ability, learning style and behaviour management. Speech and language therapists can assess the child's language and communication skills, including semantic knowledge, pragmatic skills and understanding of grammar. Occupational therapists and physiotherapists can assess the child's motor development and sensory integration and give advice on seating, feeding, and fine and gross motor development. Teaching staff can report on the child's response to school routines and the curriculum and on the child's interaction with other children. The parents can supply details on the child from birth onwards, with information on their behaviour and functioning throughout the 24-hour day, in response to different demands and environments. Health personnel can report on the child's early development and on any medical conditions. All this information needs to be assimilated, collated and disseminated to those involved with the child. When information is not shared effectively, it has limited value. There are still instances where detailed reports written by parents or professionals do not reach the teaching staff or others who are working with the child. Clear communication routes for oral and written information need to be created so that strategies and recommendations suggested are read and acted upon.

Linking diagnosis to recommendations about interventions and provision

There is little point in early diagnosis if it does not lead to educational and therapeutic advice and support for the child and appropriate support for the family. Professionals and services local to the child should be closely involved in the diagnostic process, so that the family can be supported quickly and on a continuing basis after diagnosis, and educational and therapeutic input can be planned with the knowledge and expertise which exists locally. More authorities are developing specialist diagnostic teams for ASDs so that children can be diagnosed locally. There are one or two diagnostic centres which take referrals from all over the UK, where local services do not specialise in ASDs or where there is a lack of agreement about the diagnosis. Where regional centres involve professionals already known to the child in the diagnostic process, greater consistency and continuity are ensured.

Information given to parents at diagnosis

Professionals making the diagnosis do not always provide written information or references on ASDs for the family, nor are they knowledgeable about local services. Parents still report being given no literature at diagnosis and then taking out an outdated and depressing book on autism from the local library. In some areas, agencies have produced a booklet on ASDs for the family, with details of the support available locally. Other recent publications which can be helpful include those written by the Leicestershire autism outreach team and a variety of authors in the field (Attwood, 1998; Howlin, 1998a; Leicestershire County Council and Fosse Health Trust, 1998; Jordan and Jones, 1999a; Jordan, 2001). The Mental Health Foundation has also produced a booklet for parents and carers (Mental Health Foundation, 2001) to provide information on ASDs following diagnosis.

Report writing and terminology

Use of the terms, autistic traits, autistic tendencies and autistic features

In some reports, the terms autistic tendencies, autistic traits and autistic features are used. Howlin and Moore (1997) found that of nearly 1,300 parents, 28 per cent said their children were described in these terms and were not given a definite diagnosis of autism or Asperger syndrome. Describing a child as having autistic tendencies, traits or features is not helpful, nor is it appropriate, as there is no behaviour which is unique to autism. All behaviours seen in autism are also found in the general population (Jordan and Powell, 1995). The term autistic should therefore only be applied to an individual who fulfils all the criteria necessary for a diagnosis of an ASD. In practice, it seems the terms tendencies, traits and features are used by professionals when there is evidence in only one or two areas of the triad. Some of the behaviours seen might include repetitive activity, a communication difficulty or an apparent lack of interest in other children. For these children, it is preferable to describe them along the following lines (or similar):

> the child's behaviour and skills are similar in some ways to a child with an ASD (e.g. . . .), but not in other areas (e.g. . . .). A further period of observation and assessment will be necessary to clarify the diagnosis.

Giving a parent the term autistic tendencies or autistic traits can leave them in limbo; uncertain as to whether the child has or has not got an autistic spectrum disorder. Similarly, the child might be described as having a social or communication disorder, with no mention of an ASD. Whilst such descriptions are accurate, they do not inform parents or professionals about the underlying reasons for the difficulty. There are many reasons why a child might have problems in communicating, ranging from early deprivation, trauma, sensory impairment, language disorder or an ASD and each one of these would lead to different recommendations for intervention. In addition, stating that a child has a social or communication problem alone is only describing a part of the child's functioning, to the exclusion of other aspects of the ASD, which will impact on the strategies used.

Key components of a diagnostic report

Diagnostic reports for parents and others vary a great deal in terms of their content and potential value. Good practice might include sending a copy of the draft report to parents for comment and to check with them about which people they would like copies sent to. The report should be positive and refer largely to what the child is able to do. It should also be possible for parents to recognise their child from the report, as opposed to feeling they are reading from a text book. The use of jargon should be avoided and translations should be given, where necessary. Arrangements should be made for parents with literacy problems. There should also be an opportunity for parents to return to the author(s) of the report to clarify any points made. There are a number of components which are important and some general principles which might be regarded as key to an effective diagnostic report (see Figure 2.1).

- *The basis on which the diagnosis was made (e.g. reports; observations; interview)*
- *A clear explanation of ASDs and the triad of impairments*
- *Examples of the child's behaviour which illustrate the triad*
- *Information on early development and current functioning at home*
- *Any results or scores from tests or rating scales should be explained clearly, with their implications*
- *Details of any contra-indications to a diagnosis of an ASD*
- *Areas of strength and special interests*
- *Details of other areas of development which may need addressing*
- *Key areas to focus on in the short and long term*
- *Advice on how to help the child at home and at school*
- *References to useful literature on ASDs and interventions*
- *Details of local support groups and organisations.*

Figure 2.1   Key components of a diagnostic report

In addition, care should be taken about making predictions on outcome. Recommendations on educational placement, interventions or treatment which involve other people (e.g. speech and language therapy; preschool programme) should only be made where these have been discussed with those who will be involved in funding and providing these.

Even reports which are largely concerned with explaining the diagnosis could include ideas on how parents and others might help the child, by giving references to literature and local support groups. Merely giving the diagnosis and explaining how their child's behaviour fits the diagnostic criteria, without giving any suggestions on how they or others can help the child is not as useful as it might be. The natural response after a diagnosis is to ask what can be done to help. If information and guidance is not given, parents and teaching staff may feel they are not equipped to support the child and become despondent. Many parents then do their own research and may read literature which is depressing and select strategies which are not appropriate.

Advice for parents on interventions and placement following diagnosis

The literature is clear that early intervention is important and parents should be encouraged to interact with their children from diagnosis onwards, in a way that is likely to develop skills and reduce problem behaviour (Rogers, 1996). Professionals need to deter-mine the parents' wishes and ability to engage in early intervention programmes. As a minimum, the diagnostic report might suggest ideas on how to develop the child's communication, his/her social understanding and how to use his/her special interests or favourite activities to best effect. Parents should not be made to feel they have to spend as much time as possible teaching their child. Quality of life for parents, the child and the family are crucial and the definition of this will vary between families. Parents need to arrive at their own view of how they might support the child. Many areas of the UK are setting up training programmes for parents of children with ASDs, such as EarlyBird (Shields, 2001) and Child's Talk (Aldred *et al.*, 2001), and programmes based on the Hanen programme (Sussman, 1999). An analysis of the impact of such programmes is required and an assessment beforehand on the demands made and the overall tone of the programme, using a small, pilot group of parents. There are some parent training programmes which seem too intensive in terms of the amount of information given over a short period, and others which focus mainly on deficits and difficulties, which do not inspire hope or well-being.

Giving the diagnosis to the child with an autistic spectrum disorder

There is often a focus on how the diagnosis might be given to parents, but little discus-sion on how the diagnosis might be given to the child. Much of what exists on the topic has been written by individuals with ASDs themselves. There can be no prescribed way of giving the diagnosis to the individual, as each person is different. Having said that, there are common issues that apply in most situations (Jones, 2001). It is likely that for able children, giving the diagnosis is a positive move. There will be exceptions to this and parents and professionals have to judge whether the advantages are likely to outweigh the disadvantages. What is clear is that there should be a debate between those who know the child well, as to whether to give the diagnosis and, if so, how, when and by whom this should be done.

Giving a diagnosis to those who are high functioning is likely to be important so they can develop effective strategies and explain themselves to others. Many individuals are acutely aware of their own shortcomings and their self-esteem can be very low. Giving them the diagnosis may enhance their self-esteem. It can make them aware that others have the same difficulties and enable them to join support groups or explore websites, if they wish. It can help to identify their strengths and skills and enable them to read about and meet successful people with ASDs and to make appropriate choices relating to further education and potential careers. Both Alison Hale and Gunilla Gerland feel strongly that knowing their diagnosis has been a tremendous help.

Alison said,

one of my strongest defences against all my disabilities is the awareness of exactly where my problems lie. (Hale, 1998, p. 130)

Gunilla, who was diagnosed as an adult, said that,

> it is not in our interests [to avoid giving the diagnosis] – it is not surprising that many of us end up thinking we are crazy . . . just to be able to explain to yourself why you can't do some things is very helpful. (Gerland, 1997)

There are clearly potential difficulties in giving the diagnosis to the individual and such work needs to be carefully planned and sensitively done. For some individuals, it is a relief and a largely positive experience, but for others it might lead to depression or anger, with energies being spent on challenging the diagnosis. Some might experience a mixture of emotions, both positive and negative. Where a person's initial response is anger, this does not necessarily indicate it was a mistake to introduce the diagnosis or vice versa. The first discussion will be the start of an ongoing process.

Elizabeth Newson, who has spent many years assessing children for diagnosis, argues that many children with Asperger syndrome have difficulty in listening and in the 'give and take' of discussion. She has therefore written letters to some children explaining aspects of the diagnosis and suggesting strategies (Newson, 2000). There is an advantage in sending a personal letter, as opposed to using a general booklet, as the letter can be written to suit the understanding of the individual concerned and actual examples from their lives can be used as illustrations.

There can be no set time, in terms of chronological age, that is best for giving the diagnosis, given the differences between individuals with ASDs. A Swedish team of psychologists, which has run groups for children with Asperger syndrome, say that in their experience, a child starts to ask questions about the diagnosis around the age of nine, but for some it might be younger or older than this (Wilkner Svanfeldt *et al.*, 2000). They found that children between 9 and 12 years were more actively interested than older children aged from 14 to 17 years, and suggest that the process can be started earlier rather than later.

Sharing the diagnosis with family members

Parents also need to make decisions on whether to give the diagnosis to other members of the family, both immediate and extended, and, if so, when and how. If other family members are not given an explanation of the diagnosis, they may misunderstand their brother, sister or grandchild, and become alienated from the child and angry. Some parents do not share the diagnosis as they are concerned that the child and others might use the diagnosis as an excuse (e.g. 'he can't help it, he's got autism'). Most siblings however, *know* there is something different about their brother or sister and will ask questions such as, 'Will he ever talk? Will he go to my school?' Brothers and sisters may be teased by other children for having an odd brother and so it is helpful to develop a script, as a response. The booklets produced by Davies (1995a,b) can be useful to explain some of the behaviours found in children with ASDs and Harris (1994) has written a useful book on some of the issues for siblings.

Summary

- The diagnosis of ASDs is not straightforward.
- Several professionals might be involved in the diagnostic process.
- A number of instruments have been developed for screening and diagnosis.
- Teaching staff who suspect a child might have an ASD can collect evidence on areas within the triad and contribute to the diagnostic process.
- Information for diagnosis includes past reports, information from parents on early development, observations of the child at home and at school, interviews with key staff and an analysis of the child's work.
- Parents require good information on ASDs at diagnosis and advice on how to help the child and the services which are available locally.
- Diagnostic reports need to be clear and to avoid terms such as autistic traits, tendencies and features.
- Reports which give a good picture of the child and which are positive in tone are to be encouraged.
- Discussions need to occur as to when and how the diagnosis is shared with the child and other family members.

CHAPTER 3

Educational provision

Introduction

School is one of the most challenging environments for children with ASDs because of the social demands and potential for sensory overload. Accounts from adults with ASDs confirm that schools can be confusing and frightening places. Alison Hale remembers school as follows:

> I am being transported to that place, the vast place where the screams, voices, bangs, the footsteps combine to make this painful deafening confusing mush of sound. (Hale, 1998, p. 8)

Unless pupils are helped to make order from the chaos, they are not likely to learn effectively. With a growing consensus of what seems effective, the increase in training and understanding of ASDs, and the willingness and ability of staff in special and mainstream schools to differentiate the curriculum and environment, more schools are becoming able to meet the needs of pupils with ASDs. Education authorities have responded in different ways in terms of the placements they have established and funded. Currently, a range of provision exists. Pupils might attend a mainstream school, a generic special school or a school or unit which specialises in ASDs (referred to as specialist in this book). Some education authorities will include a greater proportion of pupils in mainstream schools than others and some authorities fund proportionally more pupils in provision which is specific to ASDs. Furthermore, the practice within schools and units, even within the same category, varies with the experience and expertise of the staff. So, it is not possible to generalise about which type of placement is likely to be most appropriate for a particular child within an education authority.

Range of educational placements funded by education authorities for pupils with autistic spectrum disorders

The educational provision funded by authorities for pupils with ASDs in the UK includes:

- mainstream schools with or without extra adult support
- generic special schools or units for pupils with learning difficulties with or without additional support or outreach support

- schools, units and classes which are specific to autistic spectrum disorders
- schools or units for pupils with other types of SEN (e.g. emotional and behavioural difficulties; language disorders; sensory or physical difficulties)
- home-based programmes
- advisory/outreach teams for pupils with ASDs.

The vast majority of children with ASDs attend schools and units within their home education authority, but some attend provision in an adjoining authority and a few attend schools in a totally different part of the country, many miles from home. Most of these are run by an education authority, but some schools have been set up by independent organisations. Most of the places at independent schools are funded by local authorities, either solely by education or jointly with social services and/or health, but a few schools accept fees paid solely by the pupil's parents. Most children attend school daily, from home, but some are residential on a weekly or termly basis and a minority of pupils attend school residentially for 50 or 52 weeks of the year. Some pupils have a split placement and attend more than one school for different sessions during the week. Then there will be some school-aged pupils who are at home because they have been excluded from provision or because they have refused to attend school. They may then receive tuition funded by the education authority at home or at an educational base. In addition, some parents opt to teach their children at home themselves (known as education otherwise), and the work is monitored at intervals by the education authority.

Sharing resources on a regional basis

With the relatively recent reorganisation of education authorities, some autism-specific resources, such as outreach teams and units have been split or 'lost' to an authority. The sharing of resources between authorities therefore seems sensible. The setting up of 11 regional partnerships for SEN in England, by the DfEE, which includes all education authorities, has facilitated the discussion of issues surrounding particular groups of children, including those with ASDs. Several of the regional partnerships have chosen to look at this group and have produced reports (e.g. West Midlands Regional SEN Partnership, 2001).

Provision funded by education authorities for pupils with autistic spectrum disorders

The diversity, within and across authorities, has both strengths and weaknesses. There is strength in that different models and interventions allow variations in provision to be explored and evaluated, and assumptions about what is possible can be challenged. A disadvantage is that such variation can lead to confusion, and sometimes distress, for parents who are not able to access services they would like in their area. Given this diversity, it is helpful if education authorities provide clear guidelines on their policies and practice, and demonstrate a flexibility and willingness to listen to requests and ideas from parents and professionals alike.

The costs per pupil of each type of placement varies considerably from under £2,000 to over £130,000 a year. It is therefore essential that decisions are made which are fair to all pupils and that clear admission criteria are set out and adhered to, so that those most in need of particular provision can receive this. Calculating the actual costs of the support provided is very difficult, but it has been attempted. Jarbrink and Knapp (2001) studied the published evidence and reanalysed some of the data at the Centre for the Economics of Mental Health in London. Taking a very conservative prevalence of autism, of 5 per 10,000, they estimated the cost of autism in terms of public expenditure for children and adults in the UK as at least 1 billion annually, while the average additional lifetime cost per person was estimated to be 2.4 million.

Figures held by education authorities on pupils with autistic spectrum disorders

It is not possible to gain exact figures from education authorities as to where pupils with ASDs are placed, as records are not kept in a way which allows such an analysis. Evans *et al.* (2001) found that a third of the 74 LEAs which responded to their survey were not able to supply figures on the numbers of pupils with ASDs aged from 2 to 7 years, and of those that did, the figures were much lower than one would expect from reported prevalence studies. Previous studies which have asked education authorities or schools for figures have found the same (Jones and Newson, 1992b; Jordan and Jones, 1996). Whilst not all pupils with ASDs will have educational needs that require additional support, and the criteria for diagnosis have broadened in recent years, figures fall far short of the reported prevalence rates for ASDs. Some education authorities have conducted an audit to record how many pupils with ASDs are known to the authority. These figures can be used to support the case for the allocation of resources and also aid forward planning. The number of pupils found by age group will differ as some very young children will not yet have been diagnosed and some older pupils are not diagnosed, as a narrower definition of autism was used in the past.

Research evidence on different types of educational placement

There is little research evidence to suggest what the relative benefits are of each type of placement. Many assumptions are made in the absence of such evidence. A great deal of time and effort is expended in making decisions on school placement. Many factors influence this decision, in addition to the characteristics of the child. These include the parents' beliefs and wishes, the experience, knowledge and attitudes of teaching staff and others involved, and available provision. There is little evidence on which pupils benefit most from mainstream or specialist provision or how best to support inclusion; at the moment this must be assessed on an individual basis on what is known of the pupil's needs and the resources potentially available. There are some good examples of managing inclusion effectively (Barber, 1996; Barratt and Thomas, 1999; Parker, 2000) and of specialist schools and generic special schools creating an effective environment for pupils with ASDs (Aird and Lister, 1999; Jordan *et al.*, 1999; McCann and Roberts, 1999; Carpenter *et al.*, 2001). There have been few studies to evaluate the relative merits of different settings. Only one or two studies have compared the progress of similar pupils across different types of setting (Rutter and Bartak, 1973; Jones *et al.*, 1995). Such research is problematic for reasons discussed in Chapter 5.

To obtain data on outcomes for pupils attending different provision, it would be useful if education authorities used a tracking document (Evans *et al.*, 2001) (see Appendix 1). This would be completed on the pupil's first admission to school and then would follow the pupil and be completed at each transfer to a different school. The forms could be held centrally and data analysed at intervals to yield information on the progress of pupils with ASDs for evaluation and planning purposes within an authority and at a national level. Having good and comparable, retrospective data throughout the UK, would add substantially to our knowledge on the educational routes which pupils follow and on the outcomes at different phases of education and, ultimately, in adult life.

Schools, units and classes which are specific to pupils with autistic spectrum disorders (specialist)

Specialist provision for ASDs includes schools, units or classes which have been specifically set up for pupils with ASDs and where the majority of those on roll have an ASD. This category also includes schools which have been designated as having an ASD focus, and which may be referred to as an enhanced resource. Such schools might be a generic special or mainstream school and the school's usual catchment area might be widened for pupils with ASDs so that the school might not be the pupil's local school. Pupils with ASDs might be in classes throughout the school, with a designated room as a base (e.g. Hesmondhalgh and Breakey, 2001), or they might be taught within a specific class for some or all of their time (e.g. Parker, 2000).

It is possible to ascertain the approximate number of places which authorities provide or fund in the UK, which are specific to ASDs, from a booklet produced by the NAS. This booklet was last revised in 2000 (NAS, 2000). Information for the booklet is provided by education authorities and the schools themselves, including independent schools. The data focus largely on schools and units which have been set up specifically for pupils with ASDs or which are recognised by the education authority as having experience and expertise in ASDs. It does not include all mainstream and special schools which have pupils with ASDs on roll.

Number of education authorities which make provision specific to autistic spectrum disorders

From a survey conducted in 1988 in England and Wales, thirty (29%) of the 105 LEAs made specialist provision for pupils with autism (Jones and Newson, 1992b). This was usually a small unit for between 10 and 15 primary-aged pupils. Nine other authorities had a school within them run by the NAS or a local autistic society, bringing the percentage with specialist provision to 37%. Fifty-five LEAs (52%) did not provide any unit or school themselves which was specific to autism, but did fund one or two pupils at schools run by other LEAs or by autistic societies. There were 11 LEAs who funded no pupils at all in specialist places. Since 1988, the number of LEAs in England and Wales making their own provision has increased, and other LEAs have developed outreach services, where staff knowledgeable about autism and Asperger syndrome support staff and pupils in mainstream and special school settings. It is not possible to make a direct comparison between the 1988 figures for England and Wales and the year 2000 figures, as education authorities have been reorganised, giving a greater number of authorities (105 cf. 172), with smaller geographical areas and populations. However, of these 172 authorities, 104 (60%) have made specialist provision for pupils with ASDs, which is double the percentage found in 1988 (see Table 3.1). A further 18 authorities (10%), have an independent school which specialises in ASDs within them. However, independent schools often take pupils from a very wide catchment area and so a school might have pupils from several authorities attending, with sometimes only one or two pupils on roll from the authority in which it is sited. Fifty (30%) authorities in England and Wales were not listed as having any specialist school, unit or class for pupils with ASDs within them.

The child population (0 to 19 years) of education authorities varies a great deal from under 20,000, to over 400,000 in four education authorities in England. The number of specialist places needed will vary accordingly. Ninety-two authorities (44%) have set up more than one school or unit for pupils with ASDs. Fifty-eight (28%) of the 209 authorities had just one school or unit specific to ASDs, with 20 education authorities having 5 or 6 units or classes. A total of 315 schools, units and classes were listed, 224 in England, 50 in Scotland, 26 in Wales and 15 in Northern Ireland.

Table 3.1   Number of education authorities in the UK which have a school or unit which specialises in teaching pupils with autistic spectrum disorders

Country	Number of education authorities	Specialist ASD provision run by the education authority (EA)	Specialist ASD provision run by an independent organisation	Authority has specialist ASD provision run by the EA and independent provision	Authority has independent provision only
England	150	89 (59%)	49 (33%)	31 (21%)	18 (12%)
Wales	22	15 (68%)	2 (9%)	2 (9%)	–
Scotland	32	20 (63%)	5 (16%)	4 (13%)	1 (3%)
N. Ireland	5	5 (100%)	–	–	–
Total	**209**	**129** (62%)	**56** (27%)	**37** (18%)	**19** (9%)

Number of pupil places in provision which is specific to autistic spectrum disorders

Data on the number of pupil places were given for the majority of schools and units, and, in some cases, the number of places for those with Asperger syndrome was given separately. The reliability of the data on Asperger syndrome is not likely to be high, as some schools did not separate out this subgroup from the total figures submitted. Overall, the majority of places were said to be for those with autism. From the data analysed from the NAS booklet, the total number of specialist places available in England and Wales was 6,758, with 83% of these places within provision made by education authorities and the rest in the independent sector (see Table 3.2). When the total number of pupil places specific to ASDs was calculated in the 1988 research, there were only about 1,000 such places in England and Wales. So, this figure has increased six-fold. The total number of specialist pupil places in Scotland is 605 and for Northern Ireland is 190 (see Table 3.2). So, within the UK as a whole, there is a relatively small number of pupil places specific to ASDs (7,553), compared to the total number of children with ASDs, estimated to be about 90,000 (based on a prevalence rate of at least 60/10,000 (MRC, 2001) and a child population of 15 million in January 2001). There are places in specific ASD provision for about 8% of the child population with ASDs.

These figures give an idea of the proportion of educational provision which is specific to ASDs. But caution is needed in their interpretation. Some people, for example, might express concern that over 90% of children appear to be in provision which is not specific to ASDs. But, not all pupils with ASDs will need specialist provision. Their needs can be met effectively in a mainstream school or in other types of special provision. In addition,

Table 3.2 Number of specialist schools and units for pupils with ASDs listed in the NAS booklet (2000) and estimated number of children (0 to 19 years) with ASDs in the UK, at a prevalence rate of 60 per 10,000, plus the number of pupil places in specialist provision

Country and approx. child population (0–19 years) (January 2001)	Estimated number of children with ASDs (0–19 years)*	Schools and units run by the EA	Schools and units run by an independent organisation	Total number of schools and units	Number of places in independent provision	Number of pupil places in EA and independent combined
England 12,494,400	74,966	224	74	298	1984	6338
Scotland 1,258,300	7,549	50	6	56	123	605
Wales 744,200	4,465	26	3	29	30	420
Northern Ireland 508,200	3,049	15	0	15	0	190
Total 15,005,100	**90,029**	**315**	**83**	**398**	**2137**	**7553**

* At a prevalence rate of 60/10,000 (MRC, 2001)

there are many mainstream and special schools which are not included in these figures. They do not have a named unit or class and so do not appear in the figures given in the NAS booklet, but nevertheless, there are staff within these who are knowledgeable about ASDs and who have created effective educational environments for these pupils. There will also be some schools and units who did not submit data for the NAS booklet.

Residential provision

The majority (91%) of specialist provision set up by education authorities offer day places only, but in the independent sector, the majority of schools are residential (77%). Residential schools run by education authorities generally offered weekly boarding, with only two of these offering termly or yearly boarding. In the independent sector, many more schools offer termly or yearly boarding, with weekly boarding being in the minority. It is widely recognised that the needs of those with ASDs do not exist solely within the classroom, but are evident throughout their waking day. Both assessment and intervention have to take account of this and consider how the pupil can be supported across settings.

In many authorities, support for families lags far behind the support for staff and pupils in schools. Appropriate support services still need to be created and funded. Some children attend residential schools largely because of the needs of the family, who may have other significant demands, including other children with ASDs. In some of these cases, the child has been well supported in a day school, but there is no alternative family support available. In other cases, the residential placement is agreed largely on the severe and complex needs of the child. A range of pupils can therefore be found in residential schools. Residential schools, which provide a consistent environment are needed for the most complex children with ASDs. Good communication and common strategies across staff teams, working at different times of the 24-hour day are essential. These children are very vulnerable and need a great deal of understanding and support to function in a world that is very bewildering. For pupils who are termly boarders, there needs to be good liaison with families and flexible arrangements for contact with their child. Some residential schools have accommodation for parents on the school campus to allow overnight or weekly stays. Families can stay for reviews or to celebrate the child's birthday or spend a few hours with the child when they have returned after a school holiday. Other residential schools invite parents to training events and make home visits to exchange strategies. Residential care or short-term breaks can enable parents to maintain their equilibrium and balance the needs of all the family, so that contact with their child becomes a more positive experience for all concerned.

Units and classes for pupils with autistic spectrum disorders

In response to the particular needs of pupils with ASDs, often highlighted by parents, most education authorities have set up a specialist unit or class, with only 4% of specialist provision being in schools. In contrast, in the independent sector, there are many more schools. In terms of the host school, of the 302 units and classes, 68% were placed within special schools and 32% within mainstream settings. With increasing moves to inclusion, there is likely to be an increase in the proportion of units and classes set up in mainstream schools. Largely due to financial constraints, the staff and pupils often arrive together at the unit with little time for the induction and training of staff. Balfe (2001) writes about her experiences as an experienced mainstream teacher when she started to teach pupils with ASDs for the first time, without prior training. She describes the feelings of isolation and failure and found this was common amongst her colleagues. When establishing a new unit, attention needs to be given to geographical location; the nature, experience and attitude of the host school; the design of the environment; admission criteria; staff recruitment and training; and the preparation of staff and parents of the host school.

Age range of provision specific to autistic spectrum disorders

For provision run by education authorities, 38% of schools and units are for primary-aged pupils only, and 15% for secondary-aged pupils, with the remainder being all age. In contrast, for the independent sector, a greater percentage (65%) provide for pupils of all ages and only 11% accept primary-aged pupils. This reflects the fact that education authorities generally have more specialist provision themselves, for primary-aged pupils, and that generic special and mainstream schools may find it harder to meet the needs of older pupils. Some families also find their child more demanding in adolescence and a residential school place might be sought to support the family. Overall, at the secondary stage, there are fewer places specific to ASDs in mainstream or special schools, yet the need for such provision continues for some pupils. Further, there are some pupils who manage within mainstream primary or a generic special school, but who need more intensive, specialist support as they get older.

Number of places for adults in settings which are specific to autistic spectrum disorders

There are fewer places in adult services which are specific to ASDs. With the adult population being at least three times greater than the child population, this means that many pupils who attend specialist provision will transfer to adult services which do not specialise in ASDs. As of April 2000, there were only 1,818 places for adults with autism in the autism-specific day or residential settings registered with the Autism Services Accreditation Programme (Baillie, 2000). Although not all autism-specific services are registered, and the actual number of specialist places will be greater than this, it is clear that the majority of adults with ASDs currently attend settings that are not solely for adults with ASDs. But again, not all adults will require such a service, and many settings which have mixed populations are developing knowledge and understanding of ASDs and can offer an effective service for this group.

Meeting the needs of pupils with autistic spectrum disorders in schools for pupils with severe learning difficulties

The majority of pupils with ASDs in special schools attend SLD schools. There are also pupils with ASDs in schools and units for other types of SEN (e.g. language impairment; emotional and behavioural difficulties; and sensory impairments). Obtaining accurate figures on the numbers of pupils with ASDs in these special schools is very difficult, as some pupils will not be diagnosed and the teaching staff may not recognise the ASD. Even for those with a diagnosis, most education authorities are not able to easily extract these figures. The same is true for pupils with ASDs attending mainstream schools. It is therefore only possible to assume that given the numbers of pupils with ASDs and the number of specialist places, the majority of children with ASDs (about 90%) will attend either a mainstream school or a generic special school. Over the last ten years, with increased awareness and training opportunities, the practice within many generic special schools in relation to these pupils has been enhanced.

Meeting the needs of pupils with autistic spectrum disorders within mainstream schools

With the policy to include pupils with SEN in mainstream schools, wherever possible, and the recognition that there are greater numbers of able pupils with ASDs than was once thought, many children with ASDs attend mainstream school full-time. In addition, staff within some special schools and units provide opportunities for pupils with ASDs to spend time with normally developing children, either by reverse integration or by part-time placement at a mainstream school (Christie and Fidler, 2001). So, there are significant training implications for staff in mainstream schools, many of whom have had little training in SEN and ASDs.

Historical perspective on inclusion in mainstream schools

Separate, special provision was developed largely because it was thought that mainstream schools would not be able to address the special and complex needs of some pupils and that the education of other pupils might be adversely affected. In special provision, staff could focus on one particular area of difficulty (e.g. deafness; blindness; autism) and develop effective strategies. It was felt that children would benefit from having access to specialist staff and a specialised curriculum and that families might benefit from meeting others whose children shared a similar diagnosis. However, there has been increasing concern that separate provision, particularly special schools and units located away from mainstream schools, is not in the best interests of children and families, and that this was divisive and discriminatory (Jenkinson, 1997). In addition, separating specialist staff from mainstream teachers has meant that sharing ideas has not been easy. There is now a recognition that specialist practice does not need to be confined to a special school, but can happen anywhere, potentially.

Definitions of inclusion and integration

There have been many definitions of integration over the years and debate on how inclusion differs from integration (Sebba and Sachdev, 1997). For the purposes of this section, the following definition of inclusion is suggested to stress changes to the environment, rather than to the pupil:

> Inclusion is the process of including and educating a pupil within a local mainstream school, where the school is able to recognise and assess the pupil's particular needs and is willing and able to be flexible in how the curriculum is delivered and to adapt the routines and physical environment the pupil is expected to operate within. Particular attention is given to the relationships the pupil is enabled to develop with other pupils, both within and outside the school, and the potential benefits to other pupils and staff.

Inclusion, as defined above, would require staff training and information to understand why modifications and differentiation were necessary. It would also require strategies which created and established links with other pupils, as discussed in Chapter 6.

Expectations of mainstream staff

In some mainstream schools, pupils with ASDs have been expected to fit into existing routines and structures, and this might be insisted upon, with distressing results for the children, the staff and the families. Some staff have assumed that a pupil will eventually behave 'normally'. However, it is not possible for a pupil with an ASD to become like other pupils in many respects, and to have this expectation will lead to conflict and distress. As Clare Sainsbury, an adult with Asperger syndrome, comments, 'The problems arise not so much from Asperger syndrome itself, as from a social world not designed for people with Asperger syndrome, but for people who think and perceive the world in very different ways' (Sainsbury, 2000, p. 26).

Instead, staff need to consider the pupil's view of the situation and endeavour to differentiate tasks to accommodate the pupil's understanding and learning style. A child with a severe visual impairment would not be placed in a school without low vision aids and mobility training, yet a pupil with an ASD is often expected to manage without the equivalent support for their very particular and special needs (Jordan, 2001).

Effects of inclusion on other pupils

Some parents and teachers have concerns about the education of other children. Clearly, if a pupil is not effectively supported, then this will affect the learning environment for all. But, there are examples where other pupils have benefited and not been affected adversely. A nine-year-old, non-verbal girl with an ASD was educated in her local primary school and then transferred to mainstream secondary school (Plevin and Jones, 2000). She was supported full-time by a classroom assistant (0.8) and a teacher (0.2). Her attainments were well below those of her age peers and she was not able to read or write. She communicated with others using signs. The views of the 33 pupils in the class were obtained from group discussions. These showed the benefits they gained. The attainments of the pupils in maths and language were no different from those of pupils in the two previous year groups, which, although not conclusive evidence, is reassuring. Other pupils liked her and learned how to relate to someone who was different. The support given by the staff was crucial. At secondary school, she was given her own room in which to work, but took part in as many activities with class groups as possible. Continuing her education with pupils who knew her well was probably a key factor.

Mainstream secondary provision for pupils with an autistic spectrum disorder

The sheer number of pupils and the consequent additional noise and confusion in secondary schools can make this a very difficult environment. But, there are encouraging examples where staff have made different arrangements for pupils with ASDs, where the pupils have enjoyed success (Barber, 1996; Rocco, 1999; Barratt and Thomas, 1999; Parker, 2000). As information is shared, more pupils with ASDs might be educated within mainstream secondary schools. Hesmondhalgh and Breakey (2001) describe an integrated resource for 20 pupils with ASDs in a mainstream secondary school. They give great insight into the issues and details of the strategies they have developed. Success has been achieved for these youngsters, some of whom also have learning difficulties. Staff have arranged work experience, college placements and employment for pupils when they have left school.

Inclusion or exclusion from certain school events

Sometimes, pupils with ASDs in mainstream school have been excluded from activities and events (e.g. a visit to the Science Museum or an outdoor pursuits trip), without an adequate analysis of whether they would manage the experience and what would be needed to enable them to do so. Obviously, some pupils will need particular support during these activities, but this should not be a reason for their exclusion. In fact, this denies them an opportunity to learn new skills and further disadvantages them. Their needs should be carefully assessed and the support required provided. If excluded from events, the message to other pupils is that 'it's all right to exclude certain pupils'. Safety issues are paramount, but these should not be insurmountable and contingency plans can be made (Birkin, 2000).

Home-based programmes

In the last few years, the number of parents of preschool children wanting to follow a home-based programme such as Lovaas (Lovaas, 1987) and Option (Kaufman, 1976) has increased. Important issues arise in relation to these programmes. Key issues concern the funding, training and supervision of those who work at home with the child, how the work fits with that done by other agencies, and how the child is prepared for entry to school. Some parents have asked education authorities to fund these programmes. Such requests from parents might arise for a number of reasons, including:

- a long delay between diagnosis and the advice and interventions offered
- a lack of confidence in the provision offered by the education authority
- claims for success by the proponents of particular approaches through the media and the Internet
- a lack of specialist provision for ASDs within the education authority
- parents wish to work with their child at home in the early years.

The response of authorities to requests to fund Option or Lovaas programmes varies (Evans *et al.*, 2001). One or two education authorities have given funding directly to the parents and left it to the parents to recruit the therapists. Another authority directed parents to use a supervisor from a particular centre which education officers had checked, and the authority then employed the therapists themselves. This authority was concerned about health and safety issues, when parents appointed their own therapists whose work they were funding. Some education authorities have agreed to fund home-based programmes or other alternative provision, with the proviso that their officers can collect detailed evaluative data. Other education authorities have turned down these requests, arguing that their own provision is appropriate. These increased demands from parents, although in a minority relative to the total numbers of children with ASDs, have served to prompt education authorities to examine carefully their preschool and early provision for these children and, in some cases, to fund more staff training, more specialist posts or to increase the number of specialist places. Services for young children with ASDs in these authorities have probably improved in quality and quantity as a result of parents' requests for alternatives.

Autism outreach and advisory teams

Over the last five years, many education authorities have established outreach advisory teams, which work specifically to support mainstream and special schools working with pupils with ASDs. There might be just one outreach teacher, or several, and the team might also include an educational psychologist. These teams are an effective means of gaining an overview of provision and the needs of staff throughout the authority. Outreach staff can help teachers and others to exchange ideas and practice. Some outreach teams also provide workshops for parents following diagnosis. Awareness of ASDs and the number of children identified have often increased significantly following the establishment of the team, and ways of managing referrals and caseloads require much thought and planning, if their work is to be effective.

Choosing a school for a pupil with an autistic spectrum disorder

In the course of diagnosis and assessment, parents will generally ask a range of professionals for advice on which school would best suit their child, whether or not the professional is employed by the education authority. So speech and language therapists, paediatricians, social workers, voluntary workers, and independent psychologists might give their views on this. Where definitive statements are made by professionals, certain hopes or expectations can be generated which might not be fulfilled. This can lead to confusion and anxiety for parents. Examples of such statements are given in the following recommendations contained in reports for parents, first from a psychologist who did not have knowledge of local provision and second from a paediatrician. Neither report gave references to the literature to support these claims:

> 'In my experience, children like N require a total communication package which it is not possible to provide in a day school.' (psychologist)

> 'In our opinion, J needs to attend a school which specialises in autistic spectrum disorders.' (paediatrician)

It is especially difficult for those working in an education authority when a professional with whom the parents have a good relationship, and whom they have grown to trust, gives advice with which others working in education might disagree. This often results in the 'battles' and 'fights' with education authorities to which some parents refer. Fortunately, different agencies and disciplines are increasingly working together, so that discussions on who should advise parents on educational placement are taking place and such conflict can be avoided.

Parent partnership and mediation

The new Code of Practice (DfES, 2001) sets out the duties of the Parent Partnership Service and the responsibilities of LEAs in relation to this service (2:18). LEAs have to ensure that parents and schools are given clear information about parent partnership and other sources of support. The Parent Partnership Service can help parents during the process of choosing a school. In addition, a new service, known as the Disagreement Resolution Service, has been established, where trained mediators can help to resolve disagreements between the parents and an education authority.

Questions to ask when choosing a school

At present, a range of educational provision exists for pupils with ASDs from mainstream to special to specialist. Not all schools in the same category provide the same opportunities or interventions. Deciding which school is most appropriate in a given geographical area is a complex process. If the goal of full inclusion in mainstream was achieved nationwide, and all pupils with ASDs attended their local school, then the need for discussion about which school type would disappear. Instead, the focus would be on how the pupil was enabled to participate in the curriculum and which particular interventions to follow.

Parents need support when deciding on a school for their child. An educational psychologist is often a key person. The issue of whether formal educational assessment is required leading to a Statement or Record of Needs is often a main concern of parents. Under the new Code of Practice (DfES, 2001), a school-aged pupil with an ASD might be at any one of the three stages of assessment (School Action; School Action plus; or statutory assessment). For some pupils with ASDs, their needs can be met in a mainstream school without a Statement or a Record of Needs. The staff can devise an Individual Education Plan (IEP), in consultation with others, including the psychologist. There will be some pupils who need more help than a mainstream school can provide, from the resources normally available to them in that education authority, and a pupil might then need a Statement or a Record of Needs to obtain and secure this support. In addition, where it is thought that a mainstream school might not meet the needs of a pupil, and placement in a special school or unit might be required, a statutory assessment would need to be conducted to determine which provision would meet their needs.

Many factors determine the provision made and the pupil's characteristics alone may not be the major determinant. It is therefore possible to find similar pupils with ASDs in a range of different settings. In addition, the practice found within a particular type of school varies considerably depending on the staff, their experience, their access to training and the views and skills of visiting professionals. One mainstream school might be able to meet the needs of a pupil very well, whereas another mainstream school might not, and the same is true for special schools and units. One has to look beyond the label, and ascertain the practice and ethos within. The failure of a pupil within a school often has more to do with the features of the school and attitudes of the staff than the behaviour or characteristics of the pupil, and yet often the statement 'He failed in mainstream school' is heard, placing responsibility for the failure on the pupil.

Parents and professionals need to look at a range of possible options when trying to determine which provision would best meet the needs of a pupil. Whichever school is chosen, there will be a set of associated advantages and disadvantages. It is necessary to consider what the school is unable to provide currently and whether this can be found in some other way, either within the school or elsewhere. Schools and units differ on a number of variables as shown in Figure 3.1. These variables will be weighted differently by professionals and parents depending on their experiences and attitudes and the authority's policy. Professionals might differ in their views on what is most appropriate and parents may not agree with the authority's recommendations. Careful and considered negotiations are required to reach a consensus. For all possible schools or units potentially available to a pupil, a balance sheet could be drawn up with the parents on the advantages and disadvantages of each. Attempts can be made to reduce the disadvantages and to compare one school or unit with another, so that an informed choice is made. All schools are legally required to produce a booklet about the school, but these often do not give great detail on practice, especially on pupils with particular needs.

- *Staff expertise and experience*
- *Staff–pupil ratio*
- *The nature and amount of individual teaching*
- *The curriculum and the focus of the work*
- *Characteristics of the peer group*
- *The distance from home*
- *The nature of parental involvement*
- *Whether they are residential or day*
- *Opportunities for spending time with pupils without ASDs*
- *Access to information on ASDs or to specialist advisory support*
- *Therapy and resources available*
- *Teaching approaches used*
- *Size of classes and of the school*
- *Flexibility and differentiation to meet individual needs*
- *Staff characteristics (e.g. expertise, empathy, openness).*

Figure 3.1   Variables on which schools and units might differ

Features which are likely to create an effective placement

Parents, visiting professionals and staff who want to evaluate the potential effectiveness of a school can reflect on the extent to which the characteristics shown in Figure 3.2 are true. These features are generally considered to be important for all pupils with ASDs.

Questions on a pupil's current educational placement

When staff and a pupil experience significant difficulties over an extended period of time, it is likely that questions will be raised about whether the placement is in the best interests of the pupil. Other placements might be suggested by staff or by the child's parents. These questions can be discussed at the pupil's review. Prior to the meeting, it is important to gather clear information on which aspects of the pupil's behaviour give rise to these concerns and the extent to which strategies to address these have been devised and effectively implemented. Serious thought needs to be given to the type of help and support the pupil needs, how this might be provided and why it is felt that this is difficult or not possible within his/her current school. In addition, good information on other schools which might meet the pupil's needs should be elicited.

It is easy to imagine there is the perfect school somewhere else, but this is rarely the case. Before a placement is changed, it is important to establish how the current placement

- *Flexibility of staff to respond to the different needs of individual pupils*
- *Effective partnership with parents*
- *Calm and confident staff, who give time for pupils to process information*
- *An approach that develops from a pupil's interests and strengths rather than focusing on 'deficits'*
- *Staff who are knowledgeable and skilled in ASDs*
- *Staff and pupils who are clear on what they are doing and going to do*
- *Access to peers at an appropriate intellectual and social level, in a supportive environment*
- *A broad and relevant curriculum, which includes communication, social interaction and the development of flexible thinking*
- *Access to support from speech and language therapy, physiotherapy, occupational therapy, social services, as appropriate*
- *Support for pupils and families, beyond the usual school hours and outside term times.*

Figure 3.2   Characteristics which are likely to contribute to effective school placement for a pupil with an autistic spectrum disorder

might be modified to address the presenting problems. Exclusion should not be used as a trigger to change the placement in either mainstream or special schools. Such action often results in the pupil spending time out of school whilst another placement is sought, with the parents having to provide most of the support. This adds to the stress on the family and breaks the routine of school attendance, which might be difficult to re-establish. Where a change of placement is felt necessary, then a detailed case will need to be made to the education authority which may lead to a full reassessment of the pupil's needs and ultimately transfer to another school.

Summary

- A range of provision exists for pupils with ASDs and this varies between education authorities.
- There is little research evidence on the relative merits of different types of placement.
- It is estimated that about 8% of pupils with ASDs attend schools or units which specialise in autistic spectrum disorders, on the basis of current prevalence rates of 60/10,000.
- The majority of pupils with ASDs attend mainstream schools or special schools which are not specific to ASDs, on a daily basis.

- The main questions should not concern which school or unit the child attends, but what should be provided within the school, irrespective of type.
- More pupils with ASDs have been identified in mainstream schools and with the policy of inclusion, this number will grow.
- Professionals and parents require good information from education authorities and schools on which to base their decisions on school placement.
- A consensus is developing on the features of a school which are likely to lead to an effective placement for pupils with ASDs.

CHAPTER 4

Educational interventions

Introduction

Many different educational interventions have been devised specifically for children with ASDs or adapted from interventions originally designed for a broader population. With a growing understanding of ASDs, a consensus is developing on the types of intervention that are most likely to be effective. Given the range of needs within the spectrum, it is not likely that a single intervention will meet all the needs of an individual or that a particular approach will be appropriate for all children. There are many named educational interventions for children with ASDs. Some have been developed in the UK and others started abroad, mainly in the USA. Information on particular interventions varies a great deal and extracting relevant information on which to base decisions can be difficult and time-consuming.

This chapter focuses on named interventions, but this is not to suggest that these are preferable to methods which staff and parents have devised themselves, which often have no name and have not been publicised. The named interventions included here are currently used within the UK. It is valuable to explore the principles which underpin these interventions and how they are operationalised in practice. There are inevitably limitations, as well as potential strengths, for all interventions, and these will vary in relation to individual children. Potential strengths are given, plus questions which still need to be explored. These strengths and questions can be considered in relation to named interventions and to other interventions devised by staff and parents.

Educational interventions with pupils with autistic spectrum disorders in the UK

Some of the interventions currently used in the UK are given in Figure 4.1 in alphabetical order. It is rare in the UK for a school to adopt and follow just one approach or intervention. An eclectic approach is taken and practice is influenced by the experience and expertise of the staff and visiting professionals. It is possible for a school to be using parts or the whole of a number of interventions. It can be difficult for parents and professionals to gain information on those used within a particular school. Documents may exist on some interventions, but these are rarely collated in an easily accessible form to give an

Circle of Friends (*Taylor, 1997; Whitaker* et al., *1998*)

Daily Life Therapy (*Quill* et al., *1989*)

Intensive interaction (*Hewett and Nind, 1998*)

Lovaas programmes (*Lovaas, 1987*)

Makaton signing and symbols (*Walker, 1980*)

Musical interaction therapy (*Christie* et al., *1992; Prevezer, 2000*)

Option or Son Rise programme (*Kaufman, 1976; 1994*)

PECS (Picture exchange communication system) (*Bondy and Frost, 1994*)

Social Stories (*Gray, 1994a; Rowe, 1999*)

TEACCH (Treatment and Education of Autism and Communication-Handicapped CHildren (*Schopler and Mesibov, 1995*)

Figure 4.1 Named interventions currently used in the UK

overview of a school's work and schools change over time. A document which describes the rationale and practice of the school or unit would be very helpful. This could include sections on the theories and research which underlie the practice, a section on the approach and style taken by adults working in the school, and a section on what they prioritise for the pupils. In addition, providing evidence on the progress of pupils who already attend the school would be very useful.

When parents and teachers are told that a child has an ASD, they often ask what can be done to help. It may be assumed there is a relatively straightforward answer. Some have thought government departments for education would have a blueprint for pupils with ASDs. But, as in many areas of education, so too in ASDs, there is relatively little research evidence on which to base educational practice (Jordan *et al.*, 1998). Lincoln (1998), a Chief Education Officer, points out that there is no firm evidence base for many educational initiatives, including the National Curriculum. He therefore maintains that all those employed in education should reflect on their practice and be engaged in research activity. The Department for Education and Employment commissioned a centre whose task it is to collect and collate existing evidence in education to guide policy and practice in the future. It is known as the EPPI Centre (Evidence for Policy and Practice In education).

One of the reasons that little research has been done is that measuring outcomes, and establishing the reasons for progress, is not straightforward. Given the heterogeneity of the ASD population and the relatively small numbers of pupils engaged in particular interventions, conducting research studies and gaining conclusive evidence is not easy. The particular issues involved in research are discussed later in this chapter. Although research evidence is important, it is only one source of information that a teacher or parent might use to decide on how to work with a pupil. Knowledge of the particular child and their response to previous approaches, ideas from current theories (e.g. on ASDs, child development and learning), previous experience with other pupils and current social and cultural values, will all contribute to decisions made (Prizant and Rubin, 1999).

Making decisions on which interventions to follow

With the literature suggesting that the earlier the intervention the better, parents can feel great pressure to find the right approach quickly, which can lead to anxiety, distress and disappointment and affect their subsequent relationships with professionals they meet. Parents and staff need to make informed decisions on what they choose to do. A possible framework of questions is given in Figure 4.2.

The founders and practitioners engaged in interventions rarely have answers to all these questions, and some can only be answered in relation to a particular pupil, the family and the social context. Staff and parents may engage in an intervention without satisfactory answers to these, perhaps because they have been attracted by just one or two aspects of the approach. Greater evidence needs to be sought, so that proponents of these interventions invest more time in providing data and written information on these issues.

- *What is the rationale of the intervention and how does this fit with current understandings of ASDs?*
- *To what extent does the intervention address the needs of the pupil in the areas of communication, social understanding and flexibility of behaviour?*
- *What do the adults and child do in the intervention and how is the child likely to respond to this?*
- *What does the intervention expect to achieve in terms of outcome for the child, both in the short and the long term?*
- *What evidence is there to suggest these outcomes are achieved?*
- *For which pupils with ASDs is the intervention most appropriate?*
- *What are the financial and emotional costs and the training implications for the family and the staff?*
- *Does the intervention match the personal style of the parents or teaching staff?*
- *Is it ethical or potentially harmful to the child and the family?*
- *To what extent are the skills and understandings taught useful in a school and family context and is support given to generalise skills?*
- *Is it essential for parents to be involved and can alternative arrangements be made if this is not possible?*

Figure 4.2 Framework of questions to explore interventions for a particular pupil with an autistic spectrum disorder

Interventions offered to parents should not greatly alter their parenting style, but evolve from it. Parents can be encouraged to identify aspects of their interactions which are beneficial and develop these, whilst replacing aspects which are less successful. The same applies to staff. Decisions need to be made on whether all staff should be trained in an intervention or whether only certain staff are selected and on what basis. It is also important to ask what the intervention would replace in terms of time and resources, how easy it is to access, whether the same results could be obtained in a less costly manner, and whether the outcomes are worth the emotional and financial costs for the pupil, the family and the school. The intervention chosen should be evaluated from the start, to determine its impact on the pupil and others. On the basis of the data collected, informed decisions can be made as to whether the intervention should continue.

Research evidence on educational interventions in autistic spectrum disorders

A review of the research evidence on educational interventions in ASDs was commissioned by the Department for Education and Employment in 1998. This found that studies were often limited to those conducted by the proponents of the intervention and the majority did not include a comparison or control group (Jordan *et al.*, 1998). The studies were therefore open to bias and it was often not possible to know whether similar outcomes or better would have been achieved using a different approach. Other reviews of research into interventions have also concluded that studies suffer from shortcomings in relation to experimental design, subject selection, outcome measures, how faithfully the intervention was implemented and the interpretation of results (Freeman, 1997; Prizant and Rubin, 1999).

One of the reasons that more systematic, evaluative work has not been done is that measuring progress and outcomes in ASDs is not straightforward. The main areas of difficulty are given in Figure 4.3. Some of these are common to research on children with other SEN, but others are particularly problematic in the field of ASDs (†). In addition, it is only relatively recently that diagnostic instruments have been developed with good levels of validity and reliability, so that confidence in the populations included in past research studies has not been high.

In all studies which set out to measure the effects of an approach or placement, there are a variety of factors, in addition to the approach, which might affect rate of progress. These include the child's intellectual ability, the severity of the ASD and the length of time the child has spent in the approach. Obtaining a large sample would lessen the effects of some of these, but if a particular intervention is being studied, the numbers of children with ASDs in a geographical area is limited. Research involving a number of centres is required or data collection over a considerable time to recruit sufficient numbers. In addition, there is often a placebo effect, where children in the 'blind, no treatment group' also make significant progress by virtue of positive expectations (Lord, 2000). So one needs to be cautious in attributing progress to the intervention itself. Although research is not straightforward, it is only by engaging in research that methods will be enhanced and improved, so that decisions made can have a stronger evidence base.

- *The heterogeneity of the population†*
- *The lack of appropriate standardised measures†*
- *The difficulties in testing children with ASDs†*
- *The problem of therapist drift, as discussed by Jordan and Powell (1996), where the practice of practitioners or parents may alter to suit their personal style*
- *Professionals and parents may try more than one approach simultaneously and move in and out of approaches*
- *The knowledge and competence of practitioners can vary*
- *There may be changes in the personnel involved*
- *The nature of the approach itself may change over time as practice develops*
- *Obtaining a sample which stays within a particular research category (e.g. approach/school type/geographical area).*

† These are particularly problematic in ASDs.

Figure 4.3 Factors which create difficulties in conducting research on children with autistic spectrum disorders

Interventions used in schools in the UK

In this section, details of the most well known or commonly used named interventions in the UK are provided. They are classified in terms of whether they focus on many areas of development or on a particular area. Some of these interventions begin at the preschool stage and may be home-based initially (e.g. Option; Lovaas; PECS). They may then transfer into school. Other interventions are largely school-based in the UK (e.g. DLT; TEACCH; Circle of Friends; musical interaction). These may be shared, in part or whole, with parents, and then used at home too. Two of the interventions are parent training programmes (Child's Talk and EarlyBird), which aim to develop the child's skills by advising parents on how to develop communication and play.

To enable the reader to identify the potential advantages of each approach dealt with below and raise possible questions for research, the potential strengths of each approach are listed and questions are posed which need to be explored, in addition to those given in the framework in Figure 4.2. These questions do not only relate to the interventions described, but could be asked generally of practice within schools and units. Teaching staff reading this book could take each question and reflect on their own practice in relation to teaching pupils with ASDs.

Interventions designed to work on several areas of development and functioning (DLT; Lovaas; and TEACCH)

Daily Life Therapy (DLT) (Kitahara, 1984; Quill *et al.*, 1989)

This approach was developed in Japan in the 1960s (Kitahara, 1984) and so reflects the Japanese culture and philosophy of education. A school in Boston, USA, opened in 1987 and is run along the lines of the school founded in Tokyo in 1964. It has over 100 pupils on roll aged between 3 and 22 years, about two thirds of whom are residential. Staff–pupil ratios vary from 1:5 to 1:3. The approach used is known as Daily Life Therapy which focuses on the building of physical strength, stabilising emotions and normalising intellectual interests. The overriding principle is to establish in the pupil what is described as the 'rhythm of life' through being taught in groups, and there are few, if any, individual teaching sessions. Verbal instructions are short and concise and the children are not formally taught how to communicate. A particular focus is to ensure the pupils conform to the behaviours expected in different social situations. The pace is very fast and stimulating and there is little opportunity to engage in self-chosen or self-stimulatory behaviours. There is a very positive ethos and the children are given the strong message that they can achieve. Festivals and displays are included as part of the curriculum which offer opportunities for PE, music, drama and art. The school is very well resourced in terms of equipment (e.g. trampolines; unicycles; roller skates; musical instruments; computer and audio-visual materials). Children with epilepsy are generally not accepted at the school in case they are adversely affected by the relatively strenuous physical regime. Teaching is very formal with little practical work. Being taught to wait is an important feature of DLT.

The Principal of the Boston school reports that the pupils are not dealt with as if they were 'mentally retarded' (*sic*) and so implies that the pupils do not have additional learning difficulties. Staff therefore teach the children as a group without differentiating the work for each child. This view is not shared by other professionals in the field. There are certainly pupils on roll with severe learning difficulties and it is likely that these pupils fail to understand the verbal instructions given and the lesson content of some sessions. Many professionals from the UK have visited the school and representatives from the NAS have written two reports (Gould *et al.*, 1991; Collins *et al.*, 1995). Positive aspects reported in 1991 were successes in teaching self-care skills, the reduction in inappropriate behaviours, and the high level of skill achieved in cycling, roller skating and swimming. Differences noted in practice, when compared to UK schools, were the lack of one-to-one teaching, little work on developing communication skills and very little teaching in natural contexts. More recently, staff at the Boston school have introduced elements of other interventions, such as the visual timetables used in the TEACCH programme.

Some parents in the UK have asked education authorities to fund their child at the school in Boston. In 1998, there were 26 children from the UK on roll at the school (Jordan *et al.*, 1998). Currently, two schools have been set up in the UK following DLT principles, one of which incorporates other approaches too. Other schools in the UK have taken elements from DLT and incorporated these into their curricula. In particular, staff have introduced more physical activities into the timetable including jogging sessions and regular exercise. Daily aerobic exercise, as a way of reducing stress and challenging behaviour and improving attention, has been supported by research (Allen, 1980; Watters and Watters, 1980; Gabler-Halle *et al.*, 1993).

Potential strengths of DLT are:
- inappropriate behaviours appear to be reduced and the pupils are prepared for learning
- self-care skills and physical skills are successfully taught
- the school can provide a consistent, 24-hour programme for those pupils who attend residentially
- there is research evidence to support the benefits of physical exercise.

Questions which need to be explored in relation to DLT include:
- how do pupils manage if they have heightened sensitivity to noise and visual stimuli?
- do the tasks given match the pupils' developmental levels?
- how relevant is the curriculum for UK pupils?
- is there scope for pupils to negotiate with staff and each other?
- what proportion of pupils are able to move on to other school environments?

Lovaas programme (Lovaas, 1987)

The Lovaas programme, developed by Ivar Lovaar in the USA, uses behavioural methods to teach skills and reduce inappropriate behaviours. Behavioural approaches have been used with children with severe learning difficulties for many years in the UK and abroad, and as such, the Lovaas programme is not autism-specific. These approaches are based on the idea that all behaviour is learned and therefore appropriate behaviours and useful skills can be developed by rewarding these. In the Lovaas programme, behaviours are grouped into those which are said to be in excess (i.e. self-stimulatory behaviour; self-injurious behaviour; aggression; obsessive behaviour; and tantrums), and behaviours which are said to have a deficit (i.e. language, social skills, play skills, academic skills and self-help skills). It is argued that by using behavioural techniques, behaviours which are in excess can be reduced and those which are in deficit can be increased.

In the UK, the Lovaas programme has created a great deal of interest and attention. This has been generated as a result of the successes reported on 19 preschool children who followed a Lovaas programme for over two years, for 40 hours a week (Lovaas, 1987). At follow-up, these children had increased their IQ score by 20 points and nine of the group (47 per cent) were placed in mainstream school and described as 'indistinguishable from their normal peers'. Children in a control group who had only followed a Lovaas programme for 10 hours a week did not show gains in their IQ and all but one attended special schools. Despite criticisms about the design of this research study and its teaching methods and claims (e.g. Mesibov, 1993; Prizant and Rubin, 1999; Koegel, 2000), a number of parents in the UK have chosen to engage in Lovaas programmes.

The child is usually taught at home on a one-to-one basis by therapists trained to use the Lovaas programme and by his/her parents and volunteers. Lovaas recommends that the programme should begin at an early age, ideally before the child is 42 months old. Teaching is done for 10- to 15-minute periods and then the child is given a period of play, followed by another 10–15-minute work session. The child usually sits opposite the therapist at a table. Tasks are broken down into small steps. Clear, spoken instructions are given with physical prompts, as necessary, and appropriate responses are rewarded. A short sequence (known as a drill) is presented to teach a new target behaviour (such as sitting on a chair; looking at the adult; or repeating a word). A command such as, 'Sit down' is given and a correct response is followed by a positive reinforcer, such as a piece of popcorn or a favourite activity. The first three goals of the programme are *come here, sit down* and *look at me*. These are followed by work on imitation, matching, sorting, labelling objects, verbal imitation and preschool academic skills. Verbal praise accompanies all reinforcers so that other reinforcers can be faded out over time. If children engage in inappropriate behaviour (e.g. making noises; rocking; hitting), they are ignored or given time out. Once the child can respond correctly, without prompting, then work towards achieving mastery is done. Generalisation is said to have been achieved when skills are performed consistently in a new situation.

The Lovaas programme has attracted criticism in terms of the teaching methods used, particularly the way in which communication and language skills are worked on, out of a natural context (Prizant and Rubin, 1999; Koegel, 2000). In addition, a number of people experienced in the field maintain that the research design and methods of the main study (i.e. the Young Autism Project, Lovaas, 1987) were flawed, so that the claims made are not supported by the data (Mesibov, 1993). Howlin (1998a) also highlights the controversy on the use of the terms recovery and normal functioning, as these suggest the programme has cured the autism.

Some of the criticisms made about the Lovaas programme and its teaching methods, and claims for recovery, apply to other interventions in the field of ASDs and reflect the particular difficulties in conducting research in this area. They serve to alert practitioners to the questions which need to be asked, before embarking on an intervention. Replications of the Young Autism Project are being done in some countries, including the UK. Mudford *et al.* (2001) have reported on 85 families in the UK who had been following a Lovaas programme. Very few children were engaged in the programme for as many as 40 hours a week, the average programme being just 21 hours, and many did not have the level and frequency of supervision recommended, so a comparison of the UK data with the original Lovaas findings has not been possible, as yet.

As in other interventions, parents often modify the programme to suit their own style and the child's response, and increasingly in the UK, other interventions are used in addition to the Lovaas programme (e.g. PECS and elements of TEACCH). It is therefore important to ascertain exactly what the child is receiving, by direct observation, where possible, before passing judgement on the work in which the family or school is engaged, and before recruiting them to a research sample.

Potential strengths of a Lovaas programme are:
- early intervention
- individual teaching sessions

- structure and consistency
- the programme involves and informs parents
- parents are supported by Lovaas therapists and others who work on the programme.

Questions which need to be explored in relation to Lovaas programmes include:
- do the children become prompt dependent?
- which outcomes are chosen as measures of success?
- which elements of the programme lead to the outcomes observed?
- how are the therapists recruited, trained and supervised?

TEACCH (Treatment and Education of Autistic and Communication Handicapped CHildren) (Schopler and Mesibov, 1995)

TEACCH was developed in North Carolina by Schopler and Mesibov in 1972 and is probably the most well known and commonly used intervention in the UK. It is an approach based on the principles of structured teaching that aims to use the child's visual strengths to help them understand what is required (Schopler and Mesibov, 1995). A main principle underlying TEACCH is that if the person can see it, they are more likely to understand it and be able to do it. Workshops from the TEACCH training team in North Carolina have been held in the UK for the last 15 years, so many schools in the UK use elements of TEACCH. A number of services in the UK now have their own TEACCH trainers.

The founders of TEACCH believe in the value of having parents as co-therapists and involve them in the approach from the start, giving them strategies which they can use at home. TEACCH focuses on making instructions and expectations on the child visually very clear throughout the day, to enable them to work independently on tasks. The programme continues into adulthood and, in the USA, job coaches are employed to work alongside adults with ASDs to support them and to advise other employees on their needs and strengths. Some of the main TEACCH strategies can be grouped under four headings, as follows:

- *physical structure*: the way in which the environment is organised, be it the classroom, the home, the work place or leisure environment;
- *daily schedules or timetables:* which show the students what they are supposed to be doing and when;
- *work-systems:* which show the students what they need to do, for how long and what happens next;
- *visual instructions:* for the task itself.

Despite the fact that TEACCH methods have been used for 30 years, there has been very little research on its effectiveness and outcomes. One of the founders has reported on formal and informal measures used to evaluate TEACCH, but no major study was cited within this (Mesibov, 1997).

Potential strengths of the TEACCH approach are:
- research evidence supports the use of structure and the benefits of visual cues to those with ASDs
- it aims to teach children to work independently
- parents are supported to work together with staff on targets and programmes
- it has a long-term perspective – from child to adulthood
- it focuses on the child's strengths and interests.

Questions which need to be considered in relation to TEACCH include:
- does it reduce opportunities for interaction and communication?
- how are decisions made as to which elements of the TEACCH programme a child would benefit from?
- what is the nature of the independent work given to the pupils?
- how are TEACCH strategies transferred into the home?

Interventions designed to work on social interaction and communication skills (Intensive interaction, Musical interaction, and the Option approach)

A number of interactive approaches have been developed in the UK including intensive interaction (Hewett and Nind, 1998) and musical interaction (Christie *et al.*, 1992; Prevezer, 2000). A third approach, developed in the USA, is the Option approach or Son-Rise programme (Kaufman, 1976; 1994). They share a common rationale, but their practice differs. The proponents of intensive interaction and musical interaction have conducted research on the benefits of these approaches, but there has been no formal evaluation of the Option approach. Developing a child's ability to enjoy the company of others and to understand how to interact and communicate, is the foundation for successful teaching. This is the rationale for these interactive interventions.

Intensive interaction (Nind and Hewett, 1994; Hewett and Nind, 1998)

This was developed from work in a long stay hospital with adults with very complex needs who were not identified as having ASDs, but who probably met the criteria. These adults were often referred to as 'difficult to reach' and needed other people to meet their basic needs. Yet staff and parents could not relate to them easily, and so the importance of the work was obvious. The programme uses techniques based on early interactions between parent and child, where the actions of the individual are given meaning, through imitation and incorporation into turn-taking routines. Two key features are, acting as if the individual intends to communicate, and following not leading. The programme is intended as part of a curriculum with short daily interactions, which aim to build relationships to foster learning. It is important for the work to be done within the classroom, as the developing relationship is going to lead to other class-based activities. Video records are used to monitor and evaluate progress and data on the positive effects of this work have been reported (Nind, 1999).

Potential strengths of intensive interaction are:
- early intervention
- research evidence supports its rationale
- parents can be trained in the approach and use it at home
- it aims to develop early social and communication skills, enabling the individual to be taught other skills.

Questions which need to be considered in relation to intensive interaction include:
- how are the issues arising from close physical contact between staff and the individual addressed?
- is it too intense for some pupils?
- does it require a particular personality of staff and parents?
- how are staff trained in its use?

Musical interaction therapy (Christie *et al.*, 1992; Prevezer, 2000).

This approach was developed at Sutherland House school, a local autistic society school in Nottingham. It recognises that the development of normal communication happens through a process in which the baby and familiar adults negotiate a series of increasingly complex interactions in which the baby takes a very active part. The baby responds to the adult and invites a response and a two-way dialogue develops. The child's keyworker or parent works with the child and a musician plays an instrument to support and facilitate the interaction between the two.

Examples of the types of strategy used are:

- Tuning in to the child by joining in and copying his actions or sounds and behaving as if these were intentional attempts to communicate. Singing a running commentary song about what the child is doing (e.g. *'Ben is jumping, jumping'*.) Singing an action song which is personalised and allows space for the child to choose an action (e.g. *tickling Ben's tummy; tickling Ben's hair*).
- Leaving dramatic pauses in a song before an important key word for the child to fill in some way (e.g. with a look; sound; sign; partial word or the whole word).

There is some research evidence to support its use (Wimpory *et al.*, 1995) and it is incorporated into an early intervention package offered to parents of young children following diagnosis (Christie and Chandler, 2002).

Potential strengths of musical interaction are:
- early intervention
- research evidence supports its rationale
- adults have to observe the child very closely and take their lead from the child

- it aims to develop skills in relating to and understanding adults, which can be seen as a basis for other learning.

Questions which need to be considered in relation to musical interaction include:
- how are the issues arising from close physical contact between staff and the pupil addressed?
- is it too intense for some pupils?
- do all pupils with ASDs respond to music in a positive sense?
- does it require a particular personality of staff or parents?

The Option approach or Son Rise programme (Kaufman, 1976; 1994)

The Option approach was developed by the Kaufmans in America. They worked with their son from the age of 17 months. He is now an adult and his parents claim that he has recovered from autism. The Kaufmans maintain that it seems possible to achieve a cure using the Option approach and the word miracle appears in their literature (Kaufman, 1994). A recent brochure, giving details of their workshops, states that the Son Rise programme 'has been achieving dramatic results for over 25 years' (p. 19). No systematic or independent research has been carried out on the approach and so the evidence is limited to reports from families and the Option team themselves.

The Kaufmans run the Option Institute in Massachusetts with 20 staff and many volunteers. An important distinction is made between a person wanting a child to achieve something, and needing a child to achieve something. Option therapists firmly believe that we should want (i.e. have hopes for the children), but not need. They argue that if we need the child to talk, for example, then we must, by implication, be unhappy with the child's present state and that this unhappiness is not conducive to the child's well-being and development. Their motto is 'to love is to be happy with', but at the same time, one can be optimistic for change and work towards this.

Some parents from the UK have attended the Option Institute in America, usually funding themselves for a one- or two-week assessment. During this time, the staff at the Institute model how the parents might interact with their child and give feedback on their observations of the parents playing with the child. They also discuss ideas for play with the parents and the management of the child. On return to the UK, parents can contact the Option team by telephone and send them videos for comment. Recently, the Option team has established a centre in London so that parents no longer have to travel to the USA to be taught the Option principles.

At any one time, there is just one other person in the playroom with the child, known as the mentor. The mentor should be relaxed, happy and loving; interested in and value what the child is interested in; have energy, excitement and enthusiasm (the 3 Es); invite the child to participate in activities and achieve a balance between following the child and requesting from the child. Depending on how long the programme runs each day, there are several adults who act as mentors. These might be the child's parents or volunteers. The Kaufmans believe the ideal is for the child to have a mentor every waking hour, but this is rarely possible.

Potential strengths of the Option approach are:
- early intervention
- research evidence supports the rationale of the approach
- parental involvement and support from the Option team and therapists
- the approach values the child and where the child is now
- adults have to observe the child very closely and take their lead from the child.

Questions which need to be explored in relation to the Option approach include:
- is it too intense?
- does it promote independent play?
- does the child miss out on the experience of playing with other children?
- does it require a particular personality of staff and parents?
- how are mentors recruited, trained and supervised?

Interventions designed to develop communication skills (e.g. Makaton; PECS)

Some children with ASDs actively avoid interactions and so reduce the number of teaching and learning opportunities to develop communication skills. Even those children with good language skills often do not initiate contact and their use of language may be restricted to requesting objects and actions or protesting. The challenge is to find ways of encouraging all pupils with ASDs to initiate interactions, to become more spontaneous, to make relevant comments and ask appropriate questions (Koegel, 2000). In 1983, Prizant reviewed several programmes for developing communication and concluded that about 50 per cent of children with autism remained non-verbal. But, with increasing knowledge of ASDs and the development of interventions to encourage communication, it is thought that as many as 85 to 90 per cent of children could learn to use spoken words to communicate (Koegel, 2000).

Makaton communication system (Walker, 1980)

The Makaton system was devised in 1972 in the UK by a speech and language therapist, for use with deaf adults with severe learning difficulties. It is now used internationally with a wide range of individuals who have a variety of communication difficulties (Grove and Walker, 1990). For children with ASDs, it is thought to be more effective to use Makaton to help the child's understanding, rather than teaching the child to use Makaton as a means of expression. Many children with ASDs have difficulty in forming signs and in using them spontaneously (Attwood *et al.*, 1988). Using symbols, photos and pictures seems to be easier than Makaton and these are more easily understood by other people outside the school. Many staff use Makaton themselves alongside speech to provide an extra cue for the child and to emphasise key words.

Potential strengths of Makaton are:
- it clarifies instructions from adults to the pupil

- signs or symbols can be used by the pupil to communicate with others
- it can be taught to classmates, parents and other family members.

Questions which need to be explored in relation to Makaton include:
- what proportion of pupils with ASDs learn to use Makaton signs or symbols to communicate spontaneously?
- how are staff and parents trained to use Makaton?
- do the pupils use Makaton at school and at home?

Picture Exchange Communication System (PECS) (Bondy and Frost, 1994)

PECS was developed in the USA by Bondy and Frost (1994) who found that about 80 per cent of preschool children with ASDs had few clear communication skills. The PECS is designed to help children make clear requests for items and activities from parents, staff and others, using pictures. PECS was introduced to the UK in 1997 by Sue Baker, an educational psychologist, who is now Director of PECS in the UK. Since then, the use of PECS has spread throughout the UK and is being used in many schools. Its developers have reported studies which show the change in skills of preschool children with autism (Bondy and Frost, 1994), and studies are beginning to appear in the UK literature (Webb, 1999; 2000). As yet, these studies have not included a comparison or control group.

PECS teaches the child to exchange symbols or pictures for the objects or activities s/he would like, starting with a single picture exchange, and progresses to teaching children to construct sentences and to use pictures for commenting (e.g. *I see; I hear; I feel*). Bondy and Frost (1994) argue that giving the child a clear and effective way to communicate will also reduce problem behaviour. A critical part of the early teaching is not to pre-empt by asking, 'What do you want?' or 'Do you want a drink?', but waiting for the child to hand over the picture card first, so the child initiates the communication. The use of PECS may serve to help children understand what words are for and to learn the process of communication and develop speech.

Potential strengths of PECS are:
- early intervention
- pictures are easy for parents, classmates and other people to understand
- it aims to teach pupils to initiate communication
- it aims to progress from single picture use and understanding, to phrase and sentence construction
- it can be used into adulthood.

Questions which need to be explored in relation to PECS include:
- are skills learned at school transferred into the home setting?
- what proportion of children move beyond requesting?
- how are staff and parents trained in the approach?
- what proportion of children learn to communicate spontaneously?

- what proportion of children develop speech?

Teaching social understanding and social skills

Several methods have been devised to develop social understanding and social skills. Rogers (2000) reviewed some of the main strategies and the nature of the research evidence in this area. She noted a shift from interventions which were largely adult-directed to those which involve normally developing peers in natural settings. Most studies suggest that children with ASDs can and do develop their social understanding with age and that the role of normally developing children is very important. There is a need to develop effective measures for assessing outcome and assessing the quality of relationships, and not just social interaction *per se*. Two named interventions to develop social understanding and social skills, which are being increasingly used in the UK, are Circle of Friends and Social Stories.

Circle of Friends (Taylor, 1997; Whitaker et al., 1998)

The Circle of Friends strategy is designed to create a network of support by building links between children who are socially vulnerable and their classmates. It was not designed specifically for those with ASDs, but is being used increasingly with this group. Further details of the strategy are given in Chapter 6. It has been used successfully with pupils from the age of six upwards. Circles with pupils with learning difficulties in special school settings can be formed, possibly including mainstream pupils from a neighbouring school.

Potential strengths of Circle of Friends are:
- it aims to strengthen the relationships between the child and other pupils
- it can give positive messages about inclusion to other pupils
- it increases the number of people who can support the child within school
- it can continue beyond the school setting.

Questions which need to be explored in relation to Circle of Friends include:
- what strategies are created to support and include the pupil?
- how are staff trained in the approach?
- how can the process be continued across educational settings?
- how can the Circle be extended beyond school hours?

Social Stories (Gray, 1994a; Rowe, 1999)

Social Stories were developed by Carol Gray in the USA (Gray, 1994a) and are now used in many schools in the UK (Smith, 2001). These stories are written about a particular social situation which the pupil finds difficult, by those who know the pupil well. A specific format is used which describes the social situation and gives information on *where* and *when* the situation occurs, *who* is involved, *what* usually occurs and *why*. There are descriptive, perspective and directive statements within each story. Descriptive sentences describe what happens and where, who is involved, what they are doing and why. Perspective statements describe the reactions, responses and the feelings of others. Directive statements describe what the child should try to say or do in the situation. Gray (1994a) recommends that a social story has a ratio of between 2 and 5 *descriptive* or *perspective* sentences to each *directive* sentence. The directive sentences are best phrased as advice rather than as commands and often begin with, 'I should try . . .' or 'I may work on . . .'. Emphasis is placed on positive, acceptable actions, and sometimes giving strategies which might be used. The story focuses on the desired outcome. Rowe (1999) describes the success of a social story about lunch time written for a boy with an ASD who was refusing to enter the dining hall to eat his lunch. After hearing the story, George commented, 'Now, I'll know what to do.'

For pupils who do not find written words easy to follow, the social situation can be illustrated in the form of a comic strip. Comic strip conversations visually illustrate social situations and show the thoughts and feelings of those involved, as well as the words spoken (Gray, 1994b). Stick figures with speech bubbles and thought bubbles are used and colours can indicate emotion, with green for good and happy; red for angry or bad; and yellow for frightened. They can be used retrospectively to consider incidents and alternative endings or to think ahead as to how a situation might proceed.

Potential strengths of Social Stories are:
- they are visual (e.g. using words, symbols, photos and drawings)
- they are permanent, so the pupil can return to the story as often as necessary
- rules and expectations are made explicit
- they include statements about people's feelings and how these are linked to behaviour
- they can be used in many settings, including home.

Questions which need to be explored in relation to Social Stories include:
- for how long does the effect of a particular Social Story last?
- for how long does the strategy work for an individual?
- how are the Social Stories constructed and what role does the pupil play in this?
- can the pupil be taught to construct his/her own Social Stories?

Parent training programmes

Parent training programmes need to fit in with a family's beliefs and lifestyle so that teaching can occur in natural settings and family stress is not increased. A range of options will be necessary within a geographical area to suit the particular needs of individual families (e.g. a series of workshops; a home-based programme; literature on ASDs). Professionals need to discuss options with parents, and to negotiate and agree on needs and actions (Dale, 1996). Two recently introduced parent training programmes in the UK are Child's Talk and the EarlyBird programme. Consideration needs to be given as to what follows when the programme ends, so that parents continue to feel supported. This is made easier where those running the training are part of local services and can have a continuing role.

Child's Talk (Aldred *et al.*, 2001)

Child's Talk was developed by a speech and language therapist and her colleagues and is designed to teach parents and others how to encourage their child to communicate and interact effectively with their child. The emphasis is on empowering the parents as the key facilitators and enabling them to recognise and support their child's communication and adapt their own strategies. Therapists give the parents feedback on video records. During live play sessions, the therapist models how the parents might comment on their child's play, in a way which extends the play and develops communication. Parents are taught to recognise when and how their child is communicating and how to communicate with them in a way the child understands. They are advised to limit the number of questions they ask and to allow the child to develop his/her own play routines, on which parents can comment, but which they should not direct. They are expected to spend 30 minutes a day using these strategies. This work draws on ideas from the Hanen programme (Girolametto and Greenberg, 1986; Sussman, 1999), as does the EarlyBird programme.

EarlyBird programme (Shields, 2001)

This is a parent training programme for those with young children with ASDs who have been recently diagnosed. It suggests ways in which parents can develop communication in the home and how to understand and manage problem behaviour. It is gradually being taken up by preschool and early years services in the UK, often to supplement what is already on offer. The programme includes elements from other interventions such as TEACCH and Hanen. Those working in preschool and outreach services are eligible for EarlyBird training and it is a condition of the training that two staff from the same authority are trained together and run the EarlyBird programme as co-presenters. Six families are taken on each time for a 12-week programme. Some of the sessions are individual and home-based and others are presented to the group.

Other interventions which have implications for teaching staff

The focus of this chapter has been on educational interventions. There are other non-educational interventions which also have implications for staff and pupils. Two of these are medication and diet. Staff need to develop procedures in relation to these and ensure that these are shared and agreed within the school.

Medication

About a third of children with ASDs develop epilepsy and some need medication for this (Volkmar and Nelson, 1990). In addition, a small percentage of children with ASDs have medication prescribed to address specific behaviour problems. Such medication may have positive effects on the pupil's ability to participate in school activities, but there may also be unwanted side-effects. It is important for staff to monitor behaviours and to report back to the practitioners who prescribe. Gringras and McNicholas (1999) describe a protocol which schools can use with the GP, and Murray (1999) also provides ten guidelines which include giving the lowest possible effective dose, monitoring effects and reporting any side-effects to the prescriber. It is unlikely that one drug will affect all children in a similar way, given that the causes of ASDs are varied and children often have additional disorders. Early reports on the positive effects of medication in addressing problem behaviour and social impairments have generated false hope (Gringras, 2000). In addition, the evaluations of even the most commonly used drugs are often inadequate (Howlin, 1998b). Very few clinical trials have been conducted and great caution is required.

Dietary interventions

Research is ongoing to determine whether changing a child's diet might lead to positive changes in behaviour. The digestive system may be impaired in some children with ASDs and they may be less able to break down proteins into amino acids (Waring and Klovrza, 2000). This leads to higher levels of peptides in the gut and, as some children are thought to have a more permeable gut wall or 'leaky gut', these peptides enter the bloodstream and are thought to affect behaviour. Peptides derived from milk products (casein) and wheat (gluten) are thought to trigger some of the behaviours seen in ASDs (Shattock and Savery, 1997; Whitely *et al.*, 1999) and so some parents have excluded these from the child's diet. There have been positive reports of improved behaviour for some children and no change reported in others (Knivsberg *et al.*, 1995). Whitely and Shattock (1997) have written a short booklet giving guidance on implementing a casein or gluten free diet but stress that parents should consult their GP and/or a registered dietician before doing so. Further controlled research studies are needed, to know which children might be helped by a change of diet.

A developing consensus: common features of successful interventions

There have been a number of reviews of interventions (Harris and Handleman, 1994; Bristol *et al.*, 1996; Rutter, 1996; Dawson and Osterling, 1997; Freeman, 1997; Connor, 1998; Howlin, 1998b; Jordan and Jones, 1999b; Prizant and Rubin, 1999). These point to a growing consensus on the features of interventions which are thought to be effective (see Figure 4.4). In addition, the insights provided by adults with ASDs are extremely useful.

It follows that staff need to have knowledge of these key features and to understand why they are important. What can happen is that some staff and parents receive adequate training, but other staff and parents do not, and are expected to learn from watching others or from relatively short training sessions. They are not then in a good position to modify their approach when the pupil fails to make progress (Lubbock, 2001). Lack of

- *Intervene early*
- *Involve parents*
- *Create an environment where it is clear what the pupil has to do and which is sensitive to the pupil's sensory difficulties*
- *Develop joint attention and communication skills*
- *Allow sufficient time for information processing*
- *Gain information on the pupil's view of what is offered*
- *Use the pupil's special interests and skills and include activities s/he enjoys*
- *Include normally developing pupils in play and work*
- *Acknowledge differences between pupils with ASDs*
- *Have a functional approach to managing behaviour*
- *Support transitions within and across schools*
- *Take a long-term perspective*
- *Provide regular physical exercise*
- *Give training in relaxation.*

Figure 4.4   Features common to interventions which are thought to be successful in autistic spectrum disorders

progress or problem behaviour may then be incorrectly attributed to the nature of the pupil's difficulties, rather than to inappropriate teaching.

Questions which future research needs to address

Teaching staff and others within education authorities could conduct more research on interventions themselves, rather than being the subjects of research designed by others. Traditionally, those who work with children have been engaged fully in 'hands on' work and have had little time to evaluate their work. But, with the increasing call for evidence-based practice, and the development of outreach teams and specialist posts for educational psychologists and others, it might be possible to collect more data on the effects of interventions in the future. Some staff have already conducted research on their practice, often to fulfil requirements for higher degrees (see Burlton, 1999; Preece, 2000; Webb, 2000; and White, 2001). Such studies are valuable additions to the literature. Ideally, schools should be staffed to allow staff non-contact time to collect and analyse data. The detailed data routinely collected from IEPs, for example, might also prove useful. The main questions which need to be explored in future research are given in Figure 4.5. Obtaining data on these would help staff and parents to decide which interventions to follow.

- *What effects does the intervention have in terms of outcome for the pupil and his/her family?*
- *Which elements of the intervention are responsible for the outcomes? (e.g. intensity; content; method; parental involvement)*
- *Which pupils make the most/least progress in an intervention?*
- *What impact does the intervention have on the family?*
- *How do we support families who are not able to engage in interventions?*
- *What effect does type of school placement have?*
- *Which factors lead to the successful inclusion of pupils in mainstream school?*
- *What are the costs and benefits of engaging in an intervention (short and long term)?*

Figure 4.5   Questions that need to be explored in future research on educational interventions

Summary

- No single intervention will meet all the needs of a pupil with an ASD.
- No single intervention will meet the needs of all pupils with ASDs.
- Most schools and units in the UK use a mix of interventions in their work with pupils with ASDs, including named interventions and methods which staff have developed themselves.
- Some interventions aim to develop many aspects of functioning, whereas others have a specific focus.
- There is little research evidence on the relative effectiveness or outcomes of most educational interventions.
- Conducting research on children with ASDs is problematic due to the differences between individuals and the relatively small numbers engaged in a particular intervention.
- There is a need for teaching staff and other professionals to collect systematic data on the effects of different interventions.
- There is a need to know which elements of an intervention are effective, which children with ASDs are most suited to an approach, and whether outcomes are generalised and maintained.
- There is a developing consensus in ASDs which suggests which features of an intervention are likely to be important.

CHAPTER 5

Assessment for planning teaching strategies and managing behaviour

Introduction

Having a general knowledge of ASDs and the ways in which individuals with ASDs appear to think, perceive and understand the world is an important prerequisite for teaching these pupils. In addition, it is crucial for staff to have specific and thorough knowledge of the actual pupils they are teaching. This chapter considers how staff might gather detailed information on an individual pupil with an ASD. Ways to assess each area of the triad (as described in Chapter 1) are suggested, together with strategies on how a pupil's understanding and skills might be developed, for there is little value in assessment if it is not linked to interventions. Suggestions for the content of Individual Education Plans (IEPs) are given and issues relating to the National Curriculum and the National Literacy Strategy are discussed. Finally, there is a section on how staff might analyse challenging behaviour to devise effective prevention and management plans.

Purposes of assessment

There are a number of reasons why staff might want to assess a child. The two most common are to gain information for teaching purposes and to understand and manage behaviour. Assessments might be done to aid decisions on school placement and interventions. Staff might also want to assess the value of particular activities or resources (e.g. jogging sessions; the sensory room). Increasingly, staff are encouraged to evaluate their practice, and data on outcomes of particular interventions or on the effects of a change to the classroom might be collected. Weiss (1998) and Jordan (1999) have written useful articles on how staff might engage in different types of evaluation.

Issues in the assessment of children with autistic spectrum disorders

There has been little agreement on the most effective ways to assess children with ASDs. It has been suggested they are especially difficult to assess because of their difficulties in social understanding and interaction, their lack of interest and motivation to engage with the test materials, and an inability to work to a set time scale (Koegel *et al.*, 1997). They are likely to do best on tests which require little social interaction and which are non-verbal, with limited language demands. The results of formal assessments can be affected by the child's prior experience of formal work, their motivation, the setting, the tester's style and approach and the nature of the task, and so caution is needed in the interpretation of results.

Some children have been termed untestable, but this often reflects the nature of the measures used. Koegel *et al.* (1997) examined the variables related to differences in test outcomes for children with autism. They investigated whether the manipulation of variables related to motivation and attention would influence the child's performance. They found that modifying the procedures for administering the tests could considerably improve a child's test scores and concluded that such assessments may be testing the child's test-taking ability, rather than their intellectual or verbal ability. They suggested that the procedures for administering the tests could be altered to suit the individual's preferred style of working, provided of course the child was not helped to do the actual tasks within the test.

Methods of assessment

There are different ways in which a child might be assessed ranging from standardised tests and rating scales to structured, systematic observations or interviews and informal observations and discussions and analyses of the pupil's work. Increasingly, methods are being developed to allow pupils to self-assess and report their experiences. For standardised measures, data are available on the performance of normally developing children at different ages. The scores of a pupil with an ASD can then be compared with these. Such measures may be used to assess a child's intellectual ability, language skills, reading and other areas of development, such as self-care and independence skills. Rating scales are usually completed by those who know the child well, on the basis of existing knowledge, or as part of an assessment procedure where specific behaviours are elicited.

Teaching staff need a variety of measures, even within a specific area, because of the differences between pupils. Formal tests are often limited to a particular age group and some tests are aimed at a particular level of competence. Most standardised measures have been developed for pupils with other types of SEN and assume a normal developmental path. As such, they are not ideally suited for pupils with ASDs, whose development often does not follow the usual route. Their profile can be very uneven with some peak skills and areas where their skills and understanding are very limited. A combination of different types of assessment is likely to be necessary to give a comprehensive and accurate picture of a pupil's skills and understanding.

Assessment of intellectual ability

An assessment of the pupil's intellectual or cognitive ability can be useful for educational planning, but long past are the days when an IQ score (intelligence quotient) was a major determinant in deciding on the type of school placement. The practice of routinely measuring a pupil's IQ has declined significantly over the last 15 years and it is only a small proportion of pupils who are now assessed for IQ. Such assessments are often conducted for research purposes and may be used by some engaged in diagnostic assessment, in an attempt to determine the diagnostic subgroup.

Tests of intellectual ability are generally made up of sub-tests which assess the individual's general knowledge, visual and auditory memory, verbal comprehension and hand-eye coordination skills (e.g. Stanford-Binet (Thorndike *et al.*, 1986); Wechsler Intelligence Scale for Children – Revised (WISCIII-R) (Wechsler, 1992)). For teaching staff, the test scores themselves are less valuable than information on how the pupil carried out the tasks. It is therefore useful if the tester makes written notes on how the pupil performed the tasks in terms of their approach to tasks and problem-solving skills. Finding out how children learn is as valuable as ascertaining what they know. Information might be gained on their ability to memorise and recall different types of information, their understanding of spoken instructions, and their visual and auditory skills. Taking a video of the assessment can allow staff to analyse these areas through repeated playbacks. This is very time-consuming but may be useful in gaining an accurate picture of a pupil's skills and understandings.

Assessment of skills in different areas of development, using rating scales

Rating scales have advantages over many standardised tests and observational methods as they are relatively quick to complete, the responses are likely to illustrate the pupil's typical performance, and behaviours which are infrequent or difficult to elicit in test situations can be rated. A disadvantage of rating scales is that the information may be affected by the skills, knowledge and judgement of the rater. Training and practice in using a rating scale are important and it useful to have more than one person completing the same rating scale on a pupil, to check the level of agreement. On items where respondents differ markedly, further assessments can be made to establish whether the pupil does display different levels of skill in different settings, or whether the discrepancy is a result of a difference in how the respondents have interpreted the item concerned. An instrument often used with children with ASDs, though not specifically designed for them, is the Vineland Adaptive Behaviour Scales (VABS) (Sparrow *et al.*, 1984). This takes information from parents or key staff in four areas of development, including socialisation (i.e. relationships, play and leisure); daily living skills; motor skills and communication. It is possible to calculate standard scores and age equivalents from the raw data. The Vineland Scales are often used by researchers to evaluate the effects of particular interventions. Supplementary norms have been produced for use with children with ASDs (Carter *et al.*, 1998).

Assessment using planned, structured observations at school and home

Arguably, the most useful form of assessment for teaching staff is observation. A pupil can be observed for a number of reasons. The purpose will determine the situation observed and what is recorded. It is essential that decisions on what to look for and how to record the observations are made beforehand. Predetermined categories and coding sheets can be used or long-hand notes written which are categorised later. Staff might want to assess communication skills, social understanding or the ability to work independently, for example. They might observe the pupil during an individual teaching session, independent work, group work, whole-class work and free choice. Video and audio recordings can be valuable as these enable other staff and parents to view or hear the same situation. These allow detailed analysis of more than one aspect of behaviour and can serve as a record against which to measure progress. The type of information which can be gained from observations of the child at school includes:

- expressive ability (form, purpose, frequency and to whom addressed)
- understanding of adults' language and their responses
- percentage of time on task
- fine and gross motor skills
- nature of their interaction with other pupils
- social and cognitive levels of play
- activities which the pupil appears to enjoy
- problem-solving skills
- situations which lead to anxiety and distress.

For each one of these, it is necessary to decide on exactly what to record. This can involve considerable discussion.

Assessing the value of a school week for a pupil with an autistic spectrum disorder

It can be extremely valuable to assess 'a week in the life of . . .' or a 'day in the life of . . .' a pupil. Taking the pupil's perspective is important to ensure that they are not further stressed or distressed by what is offered and how it is offered. A pupil's timetable can be analysed to identify crisis points, and times when the pupil seems very confident and engaged. Each activity or session can be rated out of 10 on a number of dimensions, with 10 being the most positive score. Observations might focus on the pupil's emotional well-being or on how useful the session appears to be, for example. Then an analysis can be made of the high-scoring activities in terms of what they have in common. Those activities achieving a low score could be analysed along the same lines, and decisions made as to whether to shorten these sessions or whether some of the elements linked to the high-scoring sessions might be introduced to sessions that seem to work less well.

Repeated exposure and opportunities to try new activities might be needed before a real

interest and enjoyment of an activity develops. Initially, an activity might be too stimulating or confusing to be enjoyable (e.g. swimming; individual music sessions), so short
sessions, followed by a rewarding activity, can be organised which gradually build up in
duration and frequency. It is also important to consider situations outside the classroom,
at lunchtimes and breaktimes. Pupils often find unstructured times, where they are free to
choose what they do, very difficult. Many spend the time alone in repetitive activities or
routines. Others attempt to interact with peers but the interaction breaks down. They
require support from adults or other pupils to develop their social understanding and to
protect them from teasing (see Chapter 6). A useful triad of questions can be asked about
a particular activity to see how effective it is for the pupil, or these questions can be asked
about a situation where the pupil's behaviour is challenging, as follows:

- what is the pupil's view of the situation?
- what has been done to help the pupil's understanding of the situation?
- what means and opportunities has the pupil to express what s/he has experienced?

Answers to these will provide ideas on strategies to enhance the outcomes for the pupil.

Self-assessment by the pupil

Increasingly, the importance of gaining the pupil's views is stressed. Very often pupils'
opinions are inferred by others and then decisions made. Good methods for eliciting opinions which actually do reflect what a pupil feels are still in their infancy, across all types of
SEN. It seems likely that the more work staff and others do on this, the more reliable the
methods will become. If pupils are not helped to develop their ability to assess how they
feel during activities and to express choices, they will remain totally reliant on staff and
parents to choose for them. Inevitably then, there will be times when the activity or item
offered was not what the individual wanted. It is also possible that people dismiss the
choices they do make as unlikely to be real or not in their best interests. This can lead to
feelings of rejection and powerlessness. It is easy, for example, for other pupils and staff to
discount the importance of feelings which some with ASDs attach to particular activities
or objects, simply because the general population as a whole does not feel similar passions
for these themselves. If pupils with ASDs are to take some control over their lives, it is
important they are taught strategies to evaluate and report on:

- their likes and dislikes
- their strengths, interests and difficulties
- their performance on a task and the extent to which they enjoyed the activity
- their short-term needs (e.g. decisions about what to wear, what to eat, and what to do)
- their long-term needs (e.g. employment; living arrangements).

Providing a checklist of statements, starting with 'I like . . .' which have to be ticked or
marked in some way can be useful. Similarly, true/false or frequency statements about
themselves (e.g. I am a good listener; I am a calm person) where they rate 'never/ some-
times/ often' can be used (Parker, 2000). Pupils can also produce checklists of their

strengths with items such as 'I can ride a bike . . .'; 'I can feed the hens', and 'I would like to . . .' lists can be generated to help with future plans, using symbols, photos or words.

Assessment of communication

Communication can be separated into two main areas. The first concerns the pupil's ability to initiate communication and the second area relates to the ability to understand and respond to the communication of others. Many pupils with ASDs may not acquire speech (Prizant, 1983) and need to be taught alternative forms of communication using objects, pictures, symbols or the written word. They may also need to be taught the purpose of communication and how to communicate. Even those with good speech and language skills often initiate very little communication. They are usually limited too in the range of functions for which they communicate (Wetherby and Prutting, 1984). They communicate most often to request an object or activity or to try to control the behaviour of others. They are less likely to use communication for purely social ends (e.g. commenting or sharing information, greeting people and maintaining friendships) and will need to be taught the potential value of this. The speech and language therapist (SALT) is one of the key people involved in the assessment of communication. The SALT is often one of the first professionals to meet the pupil if their language is delayed. However, there is a national shortage of SALTs and some schools have limited input or no SALT for some time. To maximise their impact, most SALTs now focus on developing the skills of key staff and parents and spend less time alone with the child in assessment and therapy sessions (McCann and Roberts, 1999).

Instruments to assess communication skills

The assessment of communication skills is complex as the pupil's communicative competence varies widely in different contexts. One teacher reported being astounded at the change in the pupils' communication when they went on a residential activity holiday for a week. She then had to consider how to make the classroom a place where similarly high levels of communication were encouraged and inspired. There is a lack of reliable instruments to assess the communicative behaviour of pupils with ASDs (Lord, 1999, cited in Koegel, 2000). A number of instruments exist which have been designed for children with other types of SEN, which are used with pupils with ASDs.

Preverbal Communication Schedule (Kiernan and Reid, 1987)
This is designed for young or less able children and records all their attempts to communicate, including tantrums and actions which may not seem to have communicative intent. These can then be incorporated into interactive sessions, where they are acted upon by the adult as if the child intends to communicate.

Pragmatic Profile of Early Communication Skills (Dewart and Summers, 1988)

This is a schedule which consists of a number of everyday situations. Those who know the child well rate their usual behaviour or response. It is primarily for preschool children, but can be used with older pupils. Details are collected on the communication initiated and their responses to communication, in a range of naturally occurring situations. It is possible to assess the form in which the pupil communicates (e.g. sound; gesture; word) and the profile gives information on the purpose of the pupil's communication (e.g. requesting, protesting and commenting). It can be used as a basis for designing teaching programmes and for measuring progress.

Checklist of Communicative Competence (CCC) (Bishop, 1999)

This is designed to assess the qualitative aspects of communication in children who are known to have a communication disorder but who have sufficient language skills to speak in sentences. It is completed by those with knowledge of the child's language and communication skills (e.g. parent; teacher; speech therapist). Bishop (1998) maintains that such an instrument was needed because many children referred to psychiatric clinics with attention and behaviour problems had subtle, but significant, communication difficulties that were often not picked up. The checklist might help to differentiate the type of communication difficulty a child has (e.g. autism, semantic pragmatic or other language disorder). There are seven verbal subscales and two non-verbal scales, which look at social behaviour and interests. Examples of items are 'talks to anyone and everyone', 'has difficulty in telling a story, or describing what he has done, in an orderly sequence of events'. Each item is rated in terms of the extent to which it applies. The strengths and limitations of the instrument are discussed in a paper by its author (Bishop, 1998).

Assessment of language

Most language tests measure expressive language, verbal memory or the pupil's understanding of vocabulary and sentences. Some of the features found in ASDs would not be identified by using tests of language alone, so it is important to use tests of communicative competence as well, such as those described above. The expressive language skills of pupils with ASDs are often more advanced than their understanding of language; and their understanding of vocabulary is usually better than their understanding of grammar and sentences. As a result, a pupil's ability to understand language is often over-estimated by teaching staff, other pupils and parents. A pupil might repeat phrases spoken by others with no understanding of these (Prizant and Wetherby, 1993). For all pupils, there will be a need to assess the pragmatics of language too, that is, their social use of language, including body language, facial expression, intonation, eye contact and the ability to shift topics. These features may need specific intervention, as it is these which are likely to influence peer acceptance.

The pupil's ability to understand speech is greatly reduced when they are anxious. Adults over-estimate how much speech children with ASDs understand. This can lead to confusion and non-compliance. Research studies have advised adults to reduce the type and amount of speech they use (Lord, 1985). Potter and Whitaker (2000) studied the spontaneous communication of 18 children with autism who had minimal or no speech and found that their communication was significantly influenced by adult speech. Although staff knew they should just use key words, they found this difficult to do consistently. Where adult speech was minimal, the pupils were more socially engaged and communicated spontaneously. It is essential that staff have some means of assessing a pupil's understanding of spoken language and modify their own language accordingly, using other forms, in addition to speech (e.g. photos, symbols, written words). Three assessment tools to assess the language skills of children with ASDs are described below.

Instruments to assess the language skills of children with autistic spectrum disorders

British Picture Vocabulary Scales (BPVS) (Dunn *et al.*, 1982)
The BPVS assesses the pupil's understanding of vocabulary and can be used with children from the age of 30 months to 18 years. The pupil is asked to select which of four pictures corresponds to a word spoken by the tester. These are single words and predominantly nouns, although adjectives and verbs are included. This test provides an age-equivalent score to show the age at which a child would normally achieve a particular score.

Reynell Developmental Language Scales III (Edwards *et al.*, 1997)
These scales are often used by SALTs to assess the child's expressive skills and their understanding of language and give an age-equivalent score. They can be used with children from the age of 12 months to 7 years. The children are given set play tasks with toys and pictures and their responses to these are scored.

Test of Reception of Grammar (TROG) (Bishop, 1989b)
This assesses the pupil's understanding of grammar and identifies gaps and delays. It can be used with children from the age of 4 years to 13 years. For each item, the pupil is required to point to one of three pictures which best describes a word or phrase spoken by the tester. The simplest items are nouns, but the majority are sentences designed to test a particular grammatical construct. It provides age-equivalent scores.

Strategies to develop communication

Staff can consider the daily activities offered to pupils and analyse the number of opportunities for communication. Opportunities for pupils to negotiate, to express choices and comment need to be included. McCann and Roberts (1999) suggest the use of Joint Action Routines devised by Snyder-McLean *et al.* (1984). In this strategy, once a pupil is familiar with the sequence of a regular routine (e.g. snack time or weather reporting), the adult deliberately makes an error, sabotages part of the routine, or omits part of the sequence to provide an opportunity for the pupil to comment. A partial sequence of pictures can be shown and a pupil asked to suggest what happens next, or pictures which have a deliberate mistake (e.g. a bicycle with square wheels) may be used and pupils asked to comment on what is wrong. Even pupils with speech often initiate very little communication and taking videos of the pupil during a typical day and ascertaining the proportion of contacts initiated by a pupil, can be very enlightening. Such video records can form the basis for altering classroom routines or activities to encourage more communication.

Strategies for staff to clarify their spoken instructions

Potter and Whitaker (2000) outline the key characteristics of using a minimal speech approach as follows:

- to reduce speech to single words or two-word phrases, supported by pictures or objects (e.g. dinner; tidy; story);
- to map single words exactly onto the most meaningful aspect of the situation;
- use long pauses (5 to 10 seconds) at critical points in the interaction;
- avoid the use of questions, particularly what, why, where, which;
- delay the introduction of speech when a new task is being taught, and use physical prompts, pictures, photos and written words;
- engage in rough and tumble play and imitation of the child, leaving pauses for the child to communicate.

Staff often do not realise how much speech they are using, so it is useful to video sessions and analyse this and the pupils' responses.

Assessment of social understanding and social skills

In school, many of the demands on the pupil involve understanding the teacher's actions and intentions, and the behaviour of other children. Pupils with ASDs experience great difficulties in these areas. It is important to assess their social understanding to develop the skills they need to be effective learners in a school context. A number of ways of assessing social understanding and social skills have been devised, two of which are specifically for pupils with ASDs.

The Social Skills Checklist (Newson and MacLean, 1995)

Newson and MacLean (1995) developed a social skills checklist, which has 117 items, grouped together in four categories of conversation; following instructions and rules; concentration; and understanding emotions. Each item is marked either P for positive or N for negative, and the respondent notes YES, NO or sometimes. It is completed by parents or staff who know the pupil well. It gives information on the social skills a pupil has and identifies behaviours which interfere with relationships. Missing skills are not taught in isolation, but during the course of everyday social routines, staff would teach and encourage appropriate social behaviour and explain the reasons for social rules.

The Social Play Record (White, 2001)

The Social Play Record assesses and monitors a child's social interaction through play. It was devised by a speech and language therapist and her colleagues in a unit for pupils with ASDs within a school for moderate learning difficulties. It can be used with preschool children and into adolescence and focuses on emerging skills and interests rather than on deficits. Teaching staff, therapists and parents complete the Social Play Record based on observations and their knowledge of the child.

Ascertaining the social networks within a class

Staff can analyse the social networks within a class by observing the pupils or asking pupils to state the children with whom they usually work and play and constructing a sociogram (see Chapter 6). This information can be used to guide group membership for different activities.

Strategies for developing social understanding and social skills

Teaching social skills is very difficult as these are usually picked up incidentally from birth and not taught explicitly (e.g. when to smile; when to interrupt; to understand that people have different needs and sets of knowledge). It is important to teach social understanding, rather than merely teaching social skills by imitation. Teaching social skills alone can lead to social incompetence if the pupil does not have the understanding underlying these (Jordan and Powell, 1995). A child may be taught a social script, but be unable to adapt this if the situation changes slightly. Nor might s/he cope with the response of others who then assume greater social and communicative competence. Furthermore, what may be appropriate social behaviour in childhood may not be acceptable when the child reaches adolescence or adulthood. Pupils have to stop earlier behaviours and learn new ones. In addition, it might not be in the pupil's best interests to insist on the usual social behaviour. In relation to eye contact, for example, Gerland (1997) has said that she is unable to listen to a person if she is also looking at them. There is too much to attend to. Two strategies widely used in UK schools to develop social understanding and social skills are Social Stories and Circles of Friends. Details of these can be found in Chapters 4 and 6.

Teaching theory of mind

It has been suggested by some that teaching a child to pass theory of mind tasks might enhance social empathy and improve social skills. A book by Howlin *et al.* (1998) has been written expressly for this purpose. However, it remains to be seen whether such work does impact on general social competence. Early studies, which were relatively short term, showed that improvements in understanding emotions and beliefs did not generalise

(Hadwin *et al.*, 1997), but more research is needed. Again, one would hypothesise that working with drawings and photographs, out of a social context, might have limited value for those with ASDs, who generally need to be taught in the real situation.

Teaching pupils to recognise emotions in themselves and others

Pupils with ASDs often fail to appreciate or respond appropriately to the feelings and emotions of others. They may laugh at other people's misfortunes, possibly because they like the appearance or sound of the person who is upset or crying. They also have difficulties in recognising their own emotions. Their facial expression may not accurately reflect their own emotional state (e.g. they may not look puzzled when confused; or upset when in pain). So, they need to be taught that a variety of physical feelings and behaviours are linked to particular emotions. Drawing a child's attention to these, at the time the child appears to be experiencing an emotion (e.g. fear; anger; excitement), is likely to be more effective than simply using photographs showing different facial expressions (Jordan, 2001). Evans (1997) illustrates how outdoor pursuits can provide much material for this work. Gray (1994a) also describes strategies, where pupils rank their likely rate of anxiety in relation to a number of scenarios. For example, how anxious would the pupil feel if

> *he lost his school bag;*
> *the taxi was late;*
> *the family dog went missing.*

A strategy now commonly recommended, often by SALTs, is for staff to comment aloud on what is occurring. This can be done to explain the consequences of actions and the emotions involved. For example, 'Jason is sad because you have taken his car', or 'Sarah is excited because she is going swimming'. Some staff have used videos of TV soaps and played excerpts which vividly display certain emotions, sometimes with the sound turned off, and asked the pupils to describe the people's emotions and what might have led to these feelings. This can be a useful basis on which to develop future work. The children can create books which illustrate their own emotions (Attwood, 2000) and use a thermometer-like scale to indicate the intensity of their feelings. Lewis (1999) has used a digital camera for a variety of purposes, but reports particularly on its use to review and discuss incidents of inappropriate behaviour. She argues that if used sensitively and confidentially, in individual sessions with a pupil, they can be very effective in providing clear, visual evidence of the triggers, the behaviour and the consequences for the pupil and others, including its emotional impact.

Assessment of flexibility in thinking and behaviour

Much of the data required to ascertain the flexibility of a pupil's behaviour or thinking can be collected by informal means. The pupil's responses during everyday situations will yield a great deal of information. Staff might assess the extent to which the following are true of a particular pupil:

- resistance to a change in familiar routines

- repetitive activity with self or materials (e.g. twiddling; spinning; flicking)
- special interest followed which occupies much time and energy
- unconventional play and limited pretend play
- pursuit of own agenda and the exclusion of others' suggestions
- preference to be in control and to stay in control of what happens.

Staff need to determine whether such inflexibility is a problem for the pupil or others, or whether, in fact, it is serving an important function and can be used to good effect, as an incentive or to relax the pupil. Individuals with ASDs may behave in ways which seem odd and bizarre and can lead to people withdrawing or avoiding their presence. However, the behaviour may serve to calm the person or to block out aversive stimuli. If the behaviour is antisocial or potentially damaging to the pupil or others, then ways to manage the behaviour need to be found.

An obsession can be defined as follows:

An activity or interest in which the child engages which an adult feels is inappropriate and which may lack meaning or value to others. In addition, the activity may disturb others and limit the learning opportunities available by its nature or duration or both.

Strategies for managing obsessional behaviour

Useful questions on which to collect data to develop approaches to managing repetitive behaviours are given in Figure 5.1. Environmental factors which seem to trigger the obsessional behaviour can be changed. The pupil can be taught to communicate the feelings which lead to the behaviour (e.g. *help me; I'm frightened; I don't understand; I've finished*), using pictures, symbols or written or spoken words. Even those with speech, who know why they are anxious, may not be able to produce a statement or question to help them through a situation. They need to rehearse this with familiar adults. The pupil can be taught other ways to deal with anxiety (e.g. relaxation techniques; assertiveness training; statements or questions to 'ask' of others). It is also important for staff to check the pupil's timetable to see whether it is matched to their needs, interests and skills. Given that there are many activities within a school day which the pupil finds demanding, it is possible that their daily timetable goes from one challenging activity to another, with little respite. The more successful, confident and skilled the pupil becomes, generally the less time they will spend in repetitive activities.

Assessment of play and leisure skills

There is much evidence that children with ASDs are impaired in their ability to play in the conventional sense (Jarrold *et al.*, 1993). Their play is often repetitive, restricted and self-stimulatory, with little pretend play. It is often isolated and rarely involves others. Play is an extremely important activity for children in learning how to learn and how to interact

- *Who is it a problem for and why?*
  The behaviour may limit the pupil's opportunities (e.g. if the pupil's hands are occupied; or the frequency or duration is excessive; or it might be irritating to others). The behaviour might not be age appropriate and teasing may result. It may be dangerous to themselves or to others (e.g. running into the road to get a drain cover; breaking glass).

- *Will it be a problem later on as the pupil grows older?*
  Behaviours which are acceptable as a preschool child may not be appropriate in adolescence. In some cases, where an attachment toy or object is important, this can be exchanged for one which achieves the same outcome, but which is more age appropriate.

- *What function is it serving for the pupil?*
  Pupils may engage in repetitive activity when they are not sure what to do next. It may calm them when they feel anxious and may serve to physically block out other demands (Blackburn, 2000).

- *Could adults use this interest to positive effect?*
  The behaviour might be useful to relax the individual, to occupy their free time, as an incentive to do less desirable activities, to teach curriculum subjects using the special interest as a basis; or to develop a career.

- *How long has the pupil engaged in this behaviour?*
  Generally, the sooner adults start to manage the bahaviour when it appears, the more likely the strategy is to be effective (Howlin, 1998a). For example, when a pupil is introduced to a new environment (e.g. shopping centre; cafe; college), there is a need to be aware of behaviours which might become fixed in relation to that setting. This aspect of the experience can be altered with each visit (e.g. place to sit, the food eaten, the places visited).

- *Does the pupil engage in the behaviour at home?*
- *Is it a problem for the family?*
- *What strategies do the family use?*
- *When does the pupil usually engage in the behaviour?*
  An analysis of the settings, times of day, activities and the people present will help to identify the functions of the particular behaviour and at which times alternatives can be offered.

- *When does the pupil not engage in the behaviour?*
  Information on this aspect can prove very useful, particularly in relation to behaviours which are a response to anxiety or stress. This can identify elements which are conducive to a reduction or absence of the repetitive behaviour.

Figure 5.1   Questions to consider when devising strategies to manage obsessional behaviour

and negotiate with others. Sherratt (1999) argues that play can address the areas which are of crucial importance to children with ASDs. It may increase flexibility of thought, allow the pupil to better understand the perspective of others, and (literally) give them a role to play in relation to other pupils.

Drama allows pupils to reflect on why people think and behave in the way they do. One can experiment with different responses to a situation and examine the consequences in a safe setting. Drama can teach about empathy and emotions. For children with ASDs, current special interests, video and TV stories can all provide a theme for a drama. Two books have recently been published on play and children with ASDs (Beyer and Gammeltoft, 1999; Sherratt and Peter, 2002). Continuing to work with drama and music beyond childhood and into adolescence and adulthood also has many potential benefits. Clethero (2000; 2001), a professional singer, social worker and counsellor, writes about her work in music and drama with adults with ASDs. She and others have been amazed at the hitherto unrecognised skills of adults with ASDs in music, singing and performance.

The National Curriculum

For all pupils with ASDs, irrespective of ability, opportunities for developing communication skills, enhancing their social understanding and encouraging them to be more flexible should be an integral part of the curriculum. Most subjects within the National
Curriculum can lend themselves to work in these areas. Knowledge of the pupil's particular interests and skills can be used as an incentive to work on tasks which have less appeal.
The National Curriculum (NC) has given cause for concern to many staff working with
children with SEN, since it was first introduced in 1988. Some staff have struggled to find
activities which have meaning for pupils, under the different subject areas, and others have
felt these pupils need to spend more time on life and independence skills. Nevertheless,
many teachers and support assistants working in mainstream and special schools have been
creative and put a great deal of time and effort into providing meaningful activities within
the NC for these pupils. Seach (1998) has suggested ways in which adaptations might be
made to the National Curriculum for pupils with ASDs. The Qualifications, Curriculum
and Assessment Authority (QCAA) for Wales (ACCAC, 2000) has also produced a set of
guidelines on the National Curriculum in relation to pupils with ASDs. These include case
studies to illustrate particular teaching points and to show how pupils might be helped to
access the subject areas of English, Maths, Science, Geography, History, RE, ICT, Art,
Design and Technology, PE, PSE and Music. Advice on subject options and career choices
is necessary to ensure that pupils works towards an adult life that is feasible and person-
ally satisfying.

Assessment of reading ability

It has been estimated that between 30 and 50 per cent of high functioning pupils with
ASDs are hyperlexic, that is, they can read well in advance of their understanding. It is

therefore important not just to test the pupils' ability to read words, but to check their understanding. Their ability to predict and infer is often affected and they may not be able to identify the main theme or the most relevant details for the task. The Neale reading test (Neale, 1989) assesses both the accuracy of reading and the pupil's comprehension. It provides details on the type of errors the pupil makes and what is informing the pupil's guesses (e.g. the content, the appearance of the word or the first letter). This enables staff to devise appropriate teaching strategies. Another useful test is to read an action story, placing down pictures at the appropriate stages, and then asking the pupil to retell the story with and without the pictures. Content can be analysed and questions asked about the plot and events. This will provide details on the pupil's ability to remember the story, the meaning they take from it and whether they add their own ideas, and if so, whether these are linked to the story.

Some children with ASDs have difficulty in learning to read and in extracting the meaning and may need much more time than others to read a piece of text. Pamela Hirsch, an able woman with autism, explains how when she first reads a text, she takes almost no meaning from it (Hirsch, 2001). To understand it, she dictates the text into a tape recorder and plays it back repeatedly until the meaning emerges. So, some pupils might benefit from audio-taped stories and texts, but a quiet place will be needed.

The Literacy Hour

The National Literacy Strategy (NLS) (DfEE, 1998a) did not contain specific guidance on how pupils with ASDs or other types of SEN might access the Literacy Hour. The guidance for the Literacy Hour states that 15 minutes should be spent on a whole-class activity sharing a text, then 15 minutes focused on spelling and grammar, followed by independent or guided small group work, ending with a whole-class session to review what has been learned. Staff were concerned, initially, that pupils with ASDs would find it difficult to participate effectively in the Literacy Hour. However, some have been pleasantly surprised at the pupils' responses. Inchley (2001) identifies the following features of the Literacy Hour which are particularly suited to the needs of children with ASDs:

- it has a clear structure
- it uses visual images, texts and props
- individual teaching can be given within the small group times to work on IEP targets
- several forms of communication are used and the non-verbal aspects of stories are highlighted
- songs and rhymes can be used in a similar way to that used in musical interaction (Prevezer, 2000)
- turn-taking can be practised and paired working set up
- there is a focus on meaning
- new staff or supply staff know the system
- it is a session in which pupils can be included in mainstream classes.

Potential problems of the Literacy Hour for pupils with ASDs include the use of fictional, abstract texts, group work and group instructions, sensory overload and the pace of the group work. Drake (2001) considered how staff working within an SLD school might modify the content and format of the Literacy Hour. Modifications made were evaluated and a revised literacy strategy written, which was made available to other interested schools.

Strategies for writing and recording

Pupils with ASDs can experience problems in spelling and writing and can have motor problems and organisational difficulties. Some have dyslexia (Martin, 2002). Difficulties can arise from problems in organising and sequencing their thoughts, and in providing an adequate context for the reader. An analysis of the pupil's written work, produced under different conditions at school on a range of topics can be informative. Their written and oral language skills can be assessed, plus their ability to copy text from dictation. Some pupils with ASDs find the physical act of writing difficult and the amount and content of their written work may not reflect their overall ability. It may be difficult to read their handwriting and what is written may be relatively short. An assessment of what seems to be causing the difficulty needs to be made. Different pens or pencils and grips might be tried. Staff could ask the pupil to dictate what s/he would like to write or the pupil could use a tape recorder. Pupils often respond well to being taught to word process and being given access to a computer to record their work. Some might benefit from using voice recognition software. Pupils with ASDs are more likely to be able to write about topics of interest to them or about events they have experienced using visual prompts. They may need a list of key points and need help to plan and sequence what they write. Written work should have meaning for them and creating newsletters, lunchtime menus, celebratory cards and documents can be motivating for some.

Using computers

Computers can be a particularly effective medium for individuals with ASDs as they are visual, can be controlled by pupils to suit the pace of their processing skills, make no social demands, are predictable, do not get bored and can be intrinsically rewarding, or programmed to reward the individual (Murray, 1997). For those pupils who find handwriting difficult or become anxious when they make a mistake, word processing can help. Computers can also be used to develop communication and social understanding when shared, or by the use of e-mail and discussion groups. Some individuals have created their own websites and enjoy searching the Internet for information on their particular interests. Much still remains to be developed and discovered in using computers for teaching skills and in developing software which can be tailored to the strengths and interests of the pupil.

Individual Education Plans (IEPs)

Since their introduction in the 1994 Code of Practice (DfE, 1994), much discussion has occurred on the content of IEPs and the procedures for their construction and review. Some has focused on the areas chosen for the targets and on the number of targets to set. Both of these have been reduced in the light of experience. The IEP is not intended to document all of the pupil's needs, but to highlight priority areas which need to be taken into account throughout most or all of the pupil's activities. The new Code of Practice (DfES, 2001) states that IEPs should contain short-term targets for the child, teaching strategies and provision, criteria for success, and the date for the review of the IEP when outcomes will be recorded. It should:

> focus on three or four individual targets, chosen from those relating to the key areas of communication, literacy, mathematics and behaviour and social skills. . . .The IEP should be discussed with the child's parents. (5:51)

For a pupil with an ASD, the sensory responses of the pupil and how these might be addressed might also be included, and work on flexibility. It is useful to consider whether each of the targets is SMART, that is Specific, Manageable, Achievable, Relevant and with an appropriate Time limit. The timescales chosen will depend on the nature of the target, the needs of the pupil and what action is necessary. Targets should not remain the same for long periods. If they are not achieved, then alternative targets need to be written.

Parental involvement and contribution to IEPs

The role of parents in the construction and review of IEPs varies tremendously and ways of ensuring the full participation of parents who wish to be engaged in this work need to be found. Despite the recommendations in the SEN Code of Practice (DfE, 1994), some parents have had no involvement in their child's IEPs, and have not been given copies of the IEP (Jordan and Jones, 1996). Time for discussion in reviews is often short and it can be helpful for parents to have the opportunity before and after the review to consider what they would like to include or how they would like to contribute to the work. There is a need to train staff in writing IEPs and perhaps value in having a standard format across schools in an authority. Then pupils, parents and staff who transfer between schools do not have to learn new models. Some education authorities have produced common formats and invited the schools to use these. Figure 5.2 suggests a possible format for an IEP.

Assessment and management of challenging behaviour

Challenging behaviour is increasingly seen as a response to the demands made on the pupil and their environment, and not as an inevitable feature of a pupil with an ASD (Jordan and Powell, 1995; Howlin, 1997). As for the general population, it is generally a result of an interaction between the environment and the pupil's particular skills, understandings, physical and emotional well-being and history in a given situation. Given their impaired

A   **Summary of the nature of the child's abilities**
1   *Communication and language*
understanding of language
expressive skills

2   *Social understanding and relationships*
with adults
with other pupils

3   *Flexibility of thought*
4   *Sensory responses*
5   *Areas of strength*
6   *Particular interests (topics or activities)*
7   *Additional difficulties*

B   **Personnel involved**
1   *Internal to the school* (e.g. class or form teacher; LSA; Head of year)
2   *External agencies* (e.g. EP, SALT, SW, OT)

C   **Parents' contribution to the IEP**
1   *Targets suggested by parents, if any*
2   *Work to be done at home by parents on targets (optional)*

D   **Pupil's contribution to the IEP**
1   *Targets suggested by pupil, if any*

E   **Targets suggested by staff**
(to include targets on communication, social understanding and inclusion and flexibility)
Examples of targets:
Communication
•   *to use three objects of reference to request an item or activity (cup for drink; ball for play; tape for music)*
•   *to look towards the adult when his name is called by an adult.*

Social inclusion
•   *to set out 3 tables and 12 chairs with another pupil at lunchtime*
•   *to sit within one metre of the class group when listening to a story read by the teacher for five minutes.*

Flexibility
•   *to take his turn and perform the task displayed on the rota for making lunch.*

F   **How targets will be worked on**
1   *School staff involved* (names of staff, sessions and frequency)
2   *External professionals involved* (names of staff, sessions and frequency)
3   *Any specific programmes, materials or equipment required*
4   *Any pastoral or medical requirements* (e.g. safe haven; named teacher; medication, diet)

G   **Review arrangements**

Report to be sent to parents by: _____ *(at least 2 weeks prior to review)*

Review date: _____

Figure 5.2   Possible format for an IEP for a pupil with an autistic spectrum disorder

understanding and communication skills, pupils with ASDs will often be confused and anxious and these factors alone can lead to challenging behaviour. It is also important to consider the possibility of illness or injury as a trigger, as many individuals, even those with useful speech, may not tell their parents or staff when they are in pain. Burlton (1999) describes the deterioration in the behaviour of a young adult with an ASD. He eventually collapsed and was diagnosed as having a severely blocked intestine as a result of eating non-food items such as plastic bags.

Ways of analysing behaviour and managing the individual in a sensitive manner continue to be developed. It is often particularly hard for pupils with ASDs to change their behaviour. Those without autism are often inhibited from doing what they feel by the social consequences of their actions. They can think ahead to the likely response of their peers, the teacher and their parents. They can also read the situation to check how safe it is to engage in their desired, but illegal or anti-social or potentially dangerous, but exciting act. Will they be seen, and if so by whom, and with what result, are internal questions they might ask themselves. These will determine whether the pupil goes ahead with the action. Pupils with ASDs are less likely to go through this process or may not be held back by what others think. This is not to say that they can not appreciate the basic cause and effect principle in relation to other people's responses. They may repeat a behaviour (e.g. pinching a child) to see and hear the response of the child or the adults in the situation. It can be very difficult for them to inhibit their responses and they may not be able to indicate their confusion or distress, seek help from others, or understand exactly what it is they must or must not do (Jordan, 2001).

Clements and Zarkowska (2000) and Whitaker (2001) have written specifically about understanding and managing the behaviour of individuals with ASDs. These texts are extremely useful in assessing problem behaviour and in helping to devise plans to prevent and manage this. In their analyses, the aim is to look at the Settings, the Triggers, the Action (behaviours displayed) and the Results or response to these and then to devise an appropriate strategy. It is as important, if not more so, to work on strategies to prevent the occurrence of challenging behaviour, as it is to work out plans for managing the behaviour when it occurs. Simply reacting to incidents is not helpful to the individual or staff in the long term. Instead, staff need to modify the environment or the demands they make and work out ways to help the individual to behave differently. It is also useful to teach the pupil that certain behaviours are not appropriate or acceptable and to take responsibility for their own actions (e.g. to visually show them the consequences of different courses of action, using pictures and social stories).

LaVigna and Donnellan (1986) maintain that children with ASDs are more likely to do what is asked of them than other children and that if they do not, then it is because they have not understood the task or because they lack the skills to do it, or because for some reason, at that point, they are emotionally unable to do the task. Given the problems that those with ASDs experience with the close proximity of others and, for some, their anxiety when held, the use of physical restraint should always be seen as a last resort. Those who use physical restraint should be very well trained and supervised in its use. Similarly, medication should be used to complement other strategies and not as the sole response to challenging behaviour. One should always seek to change the environment before trying to change the brain (Murray, 1999).

Summary

- Assessment should lead to intervention.
- The purpose of the assessment will determine and inform the methods used.
- Methods of assessment include standardised tests; rating scales; structured observations and informal methods.
- Rating scales are limited by the respondents' knowledge of the pupil and the instrument, so reliability checks are needed.
- Ascertaining the value and enjoyment of the sessions offered to a pupil throughout a school day or a school week can be very useful in determining changes which may enhance their success and self-esteem.
- Methods of enabling pupils to assess their own skills and well-being and to demonstrate their preferences are still in their infancy.
- Many pupils with ASDs are able to read words without understanding their meaning, so staff need to check for reading comprehension.
- IEP targets should focus on those areas which have implications for the teaching of most skills; these are likely to include targets on communication, social inclusion and flexibility.
- IEPs should be shared with parents who can contribute ideas for targets and work on these at home, if they wish.
- Challenging behaviour is a response to the demands made on a pupil and their environment and not an inevitable feature of ASDs.
- Collecting data on the settings, triggers, behaviour and consequences of the challenging behaviour will provide a good basis for the prevention and management of this behaviour.

CHAPTER 6

Support from adults and pupils

Introduction

As autistic spectrum disorders affect many aspects of a child's life, several different services may be involved. Philippa Russell, of the National Children's Bureau, has estimated that by the time a child with a disability is five years old, the family may have seen as many as 20 professionals. It is important that good communication exists across agencies and that professionals give coherent and consistent advice. Within a school, responsibility for a child should be shared, and clear systems and opportunities to exchange information established. In addition, other pupils are a very valuable, but often under-used, resource. They can help to support the play and learning of a pupil, and in so doing, gain skills and understanding related to children who are different.

Multi-agency working

Provision from health, social services, education and the voluntary sector may be required to meet the needs of the child and the family. Traditionally, professionals in these services have worked almost independently of each other. Increasingly though, there are examples of regular meetings between planners or case workers to plan services and interventions (English, 1999). Agreeing common terms and joint working is not a simple exercise, as the focus, funding and training of each agency differ. Different disciplines work to different models (Bartolo, 2001). Some have a medical perspective and others have a social, educational or psychological perspective. So, it is unlikely that total agreement can be achieved, even in relation to the definitions and terminology used, but it is possible for each agency to have knowledge of the others' practice and rationale. Judgements can then be made as to which agencies are most appropriate for a particular child and family at a particular time. Working together, the different agencies can:

- develop a coherent diagnostic process, agree terminology and referral routes to other services, and develop systems of support and criteria for provision;
- ascertain which services are appropriate for an individual and establish who might be a named person to act as coordinator for the family;

- organise workshops for parents and professionals to increase awareness and knowledge of ASDs and offer training in particular interventions;
- make an audit of all children with ASDs within a geographical area to plan services effectively and ahead of time.

Staff training in autistic spectrum disorders

The number of professionals with knowledge of ASDs has increased tremendously in the last five years. However, there are still many who require training. Often the staff who have most contact with the children are those with the least training and experience (Helps *et al.*, 1999; McGregor and Campbell, 2001). There are instances where staff are naturally talented and do excellent work, without any formal training. Even so, they would usually welcome and benefit from information on ASDs. Many education authorities are now addressing the training needs of LSAs and setting up courses specifically for them. In most cases, though, the training is rarely given before the LSA starts working with the pupil. Training can take several forms, from within-school courses, external courses on single interventions to accredited courses. Research and practice continue to identify new approaches, so all professionals need updating. In addition, staff within schools and services change posts and so an establishment has an ongoing need for training.

Each issue of the *Good Autism Practice* journal includes information on the accredited courses currently available throughout the UK. A web-based course has recently been developed at the University of Birmingham for people with experience of working with children or adults with ASDs (e.g. parents, LSAs, residential care staff) but with few formal qualifications. This can be studied at a distance by computer from home or the workplace. Attendance at courses on particular approaches can be valuable, but these need to be supplemented by training on ASDs so that the rationale of the approach can be understood in the context of a general understanding of ASDs. Where staff do attend training events, it is important they feed back to colleagues. Before new interventions are introduced, adequate training is needed for all staff concerned, so that the rationale is understood and the intervention is implemented in the way intended. It can be the case that a child has used a system successfully in one class (e.g. PECS; a visual timetable), only to find that staff in their next class do not know how to use this or do not see its value and so it is not continued and it is denied to the child.

Assessment of training needs within a school or unit

It is important that training addresses the particular needs of participants and the setting within which they work. An assessment of training needs is therefore essential before money is invested in professional development. Ascertaining the training needs of individual staff, in the context of considering what needs to be developed on a whole-school basis, is important. Where external trainers are involved, they need to have knowledge of the work and systems used within the school and the staff's level of understanding of these, to match the training delivered to the needs of the staff. Otherwise, the impact of the training is likely to be diminished. Evaluating the outcomes of training in the workplace is also to be encouraged.

Characteristics of effective practitioners for children with autistic spectrum disorders

As the work with pupils with ASDs is increasingly documented and discussed, it is possible to make generalisations about the type of teaching style that is likely to be effective (Jordan and Peeters, 1999). These include being calm, being attracted by difference, an ability to give without getting the usual thanks, a willingness to adapt one's style of communication and interaction and never being satisfied with how much one knows. Attitudes and values are as important as knowledge and skills. It can be particularly hard for mainstream staff to appreciate a pupil has difficulties, when at times s/he appears normal and speech and academic work is age appropriate or better. Even parents report they sometimes doubt their child's diagnosis, as there are times when it is really not that evident, as is illustrated by the following comment from a mother, in a study by Carrington and Graham (2001): 'You have doubts. Does he have it? And then the next minute he does something and you know that he does.' Where staff believe a pupil is intentionally misbehaving, a power struggle can ensue, which exacerbates the situation and can lead to a total breakdown in the relationship and the placement.

Systems for sharing information within a school

Individual staff are likely to need different types of information. There are questions of who needs to know what and why, and who should decide on this. In a large secondary school, a subject teacher might teach over 300 pupils a week. Some staff might have difficulty in putting a face to a name, so a strategy where the pupil presents the teacher with written information on his or her needs might have more impact (see Barber, 1996). The teacher-in-charge of a base within a mainstream secondary school gives written information on the pupils to staff (Parker, 2000), for example: 'Ben is very sensitive about his own space. He can not bear to be crowded by anyone. Take care when you sit beside him that you are not too close. Ask him if you are in his space. If he tells you to "go away" it is usually because you are too close to him.'

Much time is spent in helping staff understand and manage the behaviour of the pupils. Their LSAs become experts at recognising the signs of stress and changing the situation to avoid challenging behaviour. Parker (2000) maintains that the pupils' presence in the school has enabled other pupils to be aware of difference and broadened the professional experience and skills of mainstream staff.

Passports to pupils with autistic spectrum disorders

Jane Jones (2000) has written about the use of 'passports' in a special school. For those pupils who are not able to tell others what they need and for those who lose the ability to communicate clearly when stressed, it can be helpful to write a passport which gives information on the activities the child enjoys and dislikes. Examples are as follows:

I like to sit on people's laps. My teachers try and persuade me to sit on a chair though as I am getting a bit big to do this now.

I hate getting dirt or paint on my hands or anything wet on my clothes and need to wash or change immediately. It really really upsets me.

Having a named staff member

It can be useful when a member of staff takes particular responsibility for a pupil. In special schools, there is often a keyworker system, where a teacher or LSA takes responsibility for two or three pupils. In a primary school, this is likely to be the pupil's classteacher and in a secondary school, the keyworker could be the pupil's form teacher, SENCO or head of year. This teacher can develop an understanding and relationship with the pupil, and act as an advocate and be responsible for collating and facilitating the information exchange between members of staff and relevant others. As the pupil's ability to understand and negotiate develops, s/he can be consulted and closely involved in decisions. Any strategies for self-assessment can be facilitated in sessions between the keyworker and the pupil.

The role of the learning support assistant (LSA)

The role of all staff is to facilitate the pupil's inclusion in work and play. Often almost sole responsibility for this is given to the LSA. But it is important that they are not the pupil's only contact at school. This will limit the relationships the pupil develops with other staff and classmates and restrict the knowledge and understanding of the pupil that others develop. Equally important, it can be a great strain on the LSA. Responsibility should be shared throughout the classroom and beyond. If the LSA spends all the time with the pupil, then the potential for 'burn-out' is high. Other support can come from classmates, older pupils, volunteers and parents.

Working individually with pupils with an autistic spectrum disorder

Given the difficulties which these pupils experience in relating effectively to others and attending to the relevant parts of a task, the work done on a one-to-one basis is a key element in effecting change and progress. Many of the current approaches advocate regular, and often intensive, individual work, where the adult is free of other children.

Working in ways which engage and maintain the pupil's interest is a challenge and requires much thought and skill. It is extremely important for staff and parents to consider how they organise individual teaching sessions, how they can deploy staff to achieve regular and reasonably lengthy sessions, free of other pupils, and how staff then structure the work. It is likely that the youngest children, and those most difficult to reach, have the greatest need for individual teaching. Staff have to make decisions on the amount of individual teaching each pupil requires within the resources available.

Factors which contribute to effective individual teaching sessions

Individual teaching sessions vary considerably in schools and units in the UK in a number of important ways. Some staff have spent much time discussing and modifying teaching sessions and a consensus has developed throughout the school. Pupils and staff can then move within the school and continue to work in a consistent manner. Figure 6.1 gives guidance on individual teaching sessions.

Observation by colleagues of individual teaching sessions

It is very useful to obtain feedback on sessions from colleagues to identify positive features and aspects which might be done differently; in particular, signals from the pupil which might be missed can be identified and taken into account next time. Although sharing video records can be anxiety-provoking, it can be extremely valuable, and one could argue that it should be a routine part of everyday school practice. Potter and Richardson (1999) acknowledge the anxieties which might arise and have given advice on how to use video in school, in a way which preserves the self-esteem and confidence of staff. Video records are also very useful in monitoring and evaluating a pupil's progress. Each pupil could have a personal videotape which is added to and used at reviews, to show the parents examples of progress, strengths, interests and any areas of concern.

Assessing the needs of the family and providing support

The needs of a family change over time as the needs of their child and family circumstances change. A range of supports are required which match the family's particular needs at different times (e.g. child-minding; short-term breaks; counselling; advice on strategies; financial support and playschemes). Asking the family what would make a real difference in terms of support is crucial, rather than anticipating what would be helpful or merely offering what is commonly given. Life at home beyond the hours of schooling, and particularly during school holidays, can be extremely demanding and greater support needs to be provided. In the course of research, parents have often expressed concern at the long school holidays, given the stated need in the literature for consistency and continuity. More support out of school hours would be welcomed by many. A mother of a child with an ASD said to me after a parent support meeting on different approaches: 'Hearing about the various interventions is interesting but what would make the most difference to me is

- *Working position within the classroom:*
  - ➤ In which area of the school or classroom will the work be done?
  - ➤ Will the adult be alone with the pupil or with other pupils and adults?
  - ➤ Will the adult have responsibility to oversee the work of other pupils?
  - ➤ Are there any potential distractions? (e.g. sights and sounds)

- *Where will the adult sit in relation to the pupil and what will this depend on?*

- *Consider the furniture:*
  - ➤ Is the working surface large enough for the activities planned?
  - ➤ Is the pupil's table or chair too high or low?
  - ➤ Can the pupil easily run off or turn his attention away from the task?
  - ➤ Do the activities demand that the pupil sits at a table or is there value in changing his/her physical position?

- *Where will the adult keep the materials for the session?*

- *What will the adult do in the session and what will this be guided by?*

- *What could the adult do to make the beginnings and endings of activities and the session clearer to the pupil to aid transition?*

- *Are the tasks relevant, realistic and useful?*

- *Will the adult use any motivators or incentives?*

- *How will the adult deal with inappropriate behaviours?*

- *Will the adult record what the pupil achieves, and, if so, how?*

- *What prompts might the adult use to increase the pupil's chances of success?*

- *Has the adult a means of evaluating his/her own performance?*

Figure 6.1   Questions to consider on individual teaching sessions

another pair of hands. I would like help to take my daughter shopping, swimming and all the other places I want to go with her.'

Many children have sleep disorders (Wiggs and Stores, 1996). They may have problems in settling down to sleep and may wake during the night or sleep for fewer hours than normal and wake early. The sleep of parents and siblings is therefore seriously disturbed. Siblings can be adversely affected as they may receive less attention from their parents, have their possessions damaged and their social life disturbed. There are positive aspects too, though, as many siblings develop a high level of skill in understanding and relating to their brother or sister and can follow careers in psychology, teaching or nursing. Literature and workshop materials for siblings are available and need to be more widely disseminated. Other factors which contribute to family stress are inadequate housing, limited finance, isolation from the extended family, lack of transport, lack of safe play areas and limited social networks.

As for any child, the nature of the support and love from parents and family members is vitally important, so it is essential that families are well supported. If the main carers are exhausted and distressed, their ability to manage the child's needs will be affected adversely. Even an able child might lack the usual self-care and independence skills, such as dressing, washing and crossing the road, and require much more supervision than a normally developing child of the same age. Forms of support for families are limited in terms of their range and quantity. Some families receive no help outside school hours; others are given one or two hours a week of support, to free the parents to do other things or to support the parent in an activity with the child. This is often only a 'drop in the ocean', and whilst parents are extremely appreciative of this, it may simply serve to show them how different their lives could be if they were given more help of this nature.

Some schools have acknowledged the needs of families and arranged to supervise and entertain the pupils out of normal school hours. A school for children with severe learning difficulties, for example, held an activities club on alternate Wednesday evenings, for pupils at the school, and their brothers and sisters, which freed their parents to go out or to simply have time alone. Another school invited its pupils to join an activities club on a Saturday morning, once a month, to allow parents free time. Some local autistic societies and other voluntary agencies have also set up sitting and befriending services. Demand invariably outstrips supply and more support needs to be developed and offered to a greater number of families nationwide. Tissot *et al.* (2001) suggest a pooling of funding and resources from health, education and social services and support from the voluntary sector to provide a package for the child and the family, so that there is continuity and consistency in provision and liaison between the many agencies involved.

Staff-parent information exchange

Throughout the literature on ASDs, the word empathy appears many times. In relation to parents, empathy is also a very important word. It is important to establish how the lives of the parents and family are affected and to offer support which is likely to be beneficial and in a way which is likely to be taken up. What is offered should not place additional stress on the parents. If parents are not getting much sleep because of their child's difficulties, they are unlikely to be in a good enough physical and emotional state to take up activities and strategies offered by staff. Staff can be disappointed and, at times, critical of parents who do not take up ideas offered. But many parents do not have the energy or resources to allow this. Very good evidence needs to be provided by staff on the potential benefits of an intervention as a prerequisite for joint working.

What can parents offer teaching staff?

Parents will have spent a great deal of time trying to understand and manage the child's behaviour. They are an invaluable resource and many parents have a library of articles, books and videos which they may be willing to lend to staff. Parents know their children intimately and have information which can be of great value to schools. Where staff invite such discussions with parents, this shows that staff are willing to listen to parents and that their views are valued. Information on health issues, on the pupil's likes and dislikes, any preferred foods and problem behaviours are important.

Without good liaison, both staff and parents might speculate on what happens at home or school and such speculation and guesswork can be inaccurate and unhelpful. Not all parents will want to be involved to the same degree or to share every aspect of the child's life at home. As one mother explained: 'If we've had a terrible time at home over the weekend, the last thing I want to do on a Sunday evening is to sit down and write about this in the home–school book.' The time, venue and frequency of contact will need to be negotiated and this is likely to vary over time. Parents should have the opportunity to speak to those in most frequent contact with the pupil, such as the classteacher, head of year and support assistant and those people may need to be freed of teaching commitments to enable this to happen.

What can staff offer parents?

Parents have often done much research on interventions and may constantly question the appropriateness and effectiveness of the placement. They need evidence and reassurance that the school is effective in meeting the child's needs. How staff respond to parents will determine how the relationship develops and how useful this partnership becomes. Hesmondhalgh and Breakey (2001) have supplied each of the 20 pupils in their integrated resource with a dictaphone. Messages and information from the staff, parents and the pupil can be communicated effectively and these have been found to work extremely well. Regular discussions between parents and key staff to check on progress and to generate strategies for particular situations are needed. Examples of good practice include:

- clear, positive, realistic written reports
- home–school diaries or dictaphones
- video evidence of what the pupil does at school
- consultation and contribution to IEPs
- home visits by staff, where parents want this

- organising support after school hours
- creating a Circle of Friends for the pupil within and outside of school
- escorts who work within school as well as on the transport
- school staff to work at home with the child, out of school hours
- transport to and from school to be offered to the parents.

Areas where staff and parents can work together include communication, self-care, behaviour management, and in creating predictable routines and less stressful environments.

Developing and enabling relationships with other pupils

Staff need to be social engineers in relation to pupils with ASDs. Adults with ASDs often describe the enormous difficulties they have in understanding social behaviour and rules. They have to consciously think about their body language and facial expressions and tell themselves to make eye contact, to smile, to alter their posture or their tone of voice. Having to consciously modify all the non-verbal elements of a dialogue is very effortful and many individuals fail to experience the pleasure of social encounters. They often express surprise that anyone would want to engage in conversation, as it seems so difficult (Gerland, 1997; Sainsbury, 2000). Others talk of being mystified by the strange social games which other humans play. Learning about ASDs helps us to understand what it means to be a social animal and how many skills we take for granted. Even able individuals, with good speech, may need a written script of what to say in circumstances where they need help from others. When they are anxious or distracted, they may not be able to articulate their wishes or realise the need to do so. They may assume that others know what they want and then feel aggrieved that this is not offered or provided.

Clare Sainsbury (2000), a highly intelligent woman with autism, commented that, 'we have been described as being in a world of our own – but we are not in a separate world at all – just paying attention to very different aspects of this one' (p. 46).

Judgements on what a pupil wishes in terms of contact with others should not be made quickly before s/he is taught how to engage with others and the potential value of this. Whilst some pupils might want to spend much of their time alone, others would like friends (Attwood, 2000).

Social subgroups within the autistic spectrum

Wing (1996a) has identified four different social subgroups, as follows:

- the aloof child who is classically withdrawn, and actively avoids social contact
- the passive child who accepts social attention from others but who does not initiate it
- the active, but odd child who initiates social contact, but gets it wrong and can not work out the social rules according to context

- the over-formal, stilted child, with good expressive skills, who may treat family members as if they were strangers.

These groups are not fixed, in that a child may move from one group to another with age and increased understanding of social behaviour.

Pupils with ASDs need to be taught by experience, that sharing an activity with others can be pleasurable, as they will not easily arrive at this realisation themselves. Some of the social encounters they experience with others are unpleasant and anxiety-provoking. There are some individuals who genuinely prefer to spend most of their time alone and this should be respected. Within the general population, the ways in which people choose to live, varies considerably and value judgements should be avoided in relation to those with ASDs.

Simplistic notions of friendship

Pupils need to be taught the skills of starting a friendship and maintaining this. Some have a very simplistic notion of what one needs to do to gain a friend and what friendship entails (Attwood, 2000). One able pupil said, 'I thought all I had to do was to go up to a group of boys and start talking.' He would approach them and talk about the planets. He did not realise he had to listen to the topic and choose an appropriate moment and a relevant comment to join the conversation. As a result, he was either teased or ignored and could not understand why. When pupils or staff criticised him, they either used humour, which he failed to understand, or they were brutally honest, which upset him. He did not understand conversations between peers and how they arrived at common understandings and jokes. Staff tried to teach him some of the rules for playing, but he thought school was for maths and science and could not understand why his teachers were spending time on play. It is important not just to teach children with ASDs the social rules, but to explain the reasons for them. If they do not understand the reasons, they may do the wrong thing when the situation changes. Social Stories (Gray, 1994a) can be used for this purpose (see Chapter 4). Care has to be taken that the rules always apply, or that the times when the rules do not apply are made explicit, as the pupils will not have the flexibility to adapt these, when necessary.

Bullying and teasing

Parents with children in mainstream settings are often particularly concerned about potential bullying (Hesmondhalgh and Breakey, 2001). Accounts from adults often report a great deal of teasing and bullying at school (Gerland, 1997; Sainsbury, 2000). This issue is not confined to mainstream schools though, and pupils in all types of school need protection. Good supervision and effective whole-school anti-bullying policies are required, with clear procedures for the pupils to follow when they experience or witness acts of bullying. It is as important, and more likely to be effective, to change the behaviour of other pupils, than to spend time solely on teaching the child with an ASD how to manage teasing. Pupils can be taught assertiveness skills and what to do, possibly through role-play or Social Stories (Gray, 1994a). They might find it difficult to report on which pupils are involved in incidents though, as they may not recognise or be able to name the perpetrators. Gerland (1997) reported that she was unable to tell staff which pupils had bullied her, as 'they all had boy faces'. Similarly, Clare Sainsbury (2000) said that she would confuse children with the same hair colour or haircut.

Assessment of social relationships

There are often other pupils, as well as the pupil with an ASD, who require support to be socially included. To determine the social networks within a class, a sociogram can be constructed which illustrates the social links between pupils and whether these are reciprocated. Usually, the classteacher would ask the pupils to write down the names of two pupils with whom they would choose to work and play. Alternatively, each pupil can be given the class list and asked to record which pupils they spend time with, in terms of frequency, ranging from none to a great deal. For pupils who are unable to express a choice, staff can make observations and note down the number and type of interactions the pupil initiates and receives. Staff could shadow the pupil throughout the school day to analyse the nature of contact with others and his/her emotional response to this. Hyde *et al.* (2001) describe the use of an instrument for preschool children, known as the Coding of Active Sociability in Preschoolers with Autism schedule (CASPA). Sessions of free play and specific play situations in natural settings are videoed. Incidents where the child seems most sociable are analysed to devise strategies that might increase their social play and understanding. This could be extended for use with older pupils.

Given the relatively high degree of adult support which many pupils require and receive, there is a danger that they can become very adult focused, and rarely interact with other pupils. They often relate more easily to adults than to pupils, as adults are more likely to compensate for their difficulties. It is therefore necessary to deliberately engineer contact with classmates. 'Everybody knew Joe, but he had no friends' is a quote from a support teacher about a pupil in a mainstream secondary school. This illustrates what can happen unless specific work is done to foster interactions with other pupils. Joe was very amenable and had the potential to be included in activities with other pupils (as he did with his siblings at home), but no work in school had been done to facilitate this. The focus had been solely on his academic work. Staff can ask parents about the nature of the pupil's social contacts outside school with family members and friends. Often at reviews, parents report that the pupil has no friends outside the family. Where a person spends many waking hours alone, they may engage in negative thoughts which are hard to shift in the absence of alternative activities or interactions with others.

Developing social interaction with pupils in mainstream schools

One of the potential strengths of attending a mainstream school is the opportunity for pupils with ASDs to work with children with relatively good social and communication skills. The degree to which this opportunity is acted upon and capitalised varies from school to school. Some classmates find ways of engaging the pupil with an ASD without any adult intervention, but in most cases teaching staff will need to encourage and support mainstream pupils in this, during classwork and at break times. Without help, the pupil will often remain isolated.

Other pupils can act as additional resources within the classroom and so reduce the demands made on staff time. One can enlarge the number of people to support the pupil from one or two adults in the class to include five or six pupils, who in turn can instruct other pupils what to do. They can direct the pupil's attention to the task, or model what should be done next. They can learn the pupil's signs or other methods of communication. Some pupils, through a Circle of Friends, have given a signal to the focus child (e.g. a whistle, certain phrase, hand signal), when they notice the child is about to do something inappropriate or is 'going too far'. Pupils can be very creative in discussing how a pupil might be enabled to join an activity or to overcome a problem, and strategies which the pupils devise might have more chance of success than those suggested by staff.

Sharing information about a pupil with an autistic spectrum disorder with peers

Some staff and parents may choose not to formally share information about ASDs or about the pupil with the rest of the class. They prefer questions to be dealt with as and when they arise. Others feel it is useful to talk to the whole class. There is no prescribed method for presenting such information. It will depend to an extent on the skills and experience of those involved. A variety of strategies have been used. These include presentations by the pupil's parents or siblings, using photographs and videos. The diagnosis might not be mentioned *per se*, but a discussion on how the pupil is different and on his/her strengths or positive qualities might be helpful. Teachers from within the school or the outreach team can also talk to the class. Where a Circle of Friends has been formed, other pupils in the Circle can informally teach their classmates about the pupil. Campbell and Gregory (2000) have created a set of books for children to explain autism, one of which is entitled, *Someone I know has autism*, and this set of books can be used with classmates.

Social relationships with siblings

Knott *et al.* (1995) found that children with autism generally played more easily with their brothers and sisters than they did with other children. The siblings had acquired knowledge and skills which other children did not possess. It is likely that their parents had played a significant role in teaching them how to interact with the child and how to maintain the interaction. This suggests that other pupils in a school context can be taught to play successfully with pupils with ASDs. Children learn a tremendous amount from the sibling relationship. They learn to negotiate, to fight, to make up, to share and to cooperate. O'Connell (1999) describes the positive effect of her younger daughter on developing the social understanding of her seven-year-old son with an ASD. Teaching staff can gain useful information from parents on the ways in which the child plays and interacts with brothers and sisters which can guide them in how to support peer relationships in school. Games for preschool children can include ball games, Lego, telephones, singing and action tapes, balloons, bubbles and water. For school-age children, cooking, board games, dominoes, football and card games work well. In adolescence, cooking, shopping, outdoor pursuits, listening to music, snooker, art and crafts and card games are possible activities.

Group work in the classroom for pupils with autistic spectrum disorders

Given the difficulties that pupils have in understanding and relating effectively with others, careful thought needs to be given as to how working with others is best organised. It will usually be necessary to progress sensitively and gradually towards working as one of a group. Initially, the pupil can be taught alongside other pupils, but at an appropriate distance from them. Some may benefit from having a toy or other distracter to focus on. Gradually, the distance between the child and other pupils can be reduced. Working with just one other pupil on a suitable and familiar activity would be a useful step on the way to small group work. For some children, the social demands will greatly interfere with their ability to perform the academic task. It is generally preferable, when introducing the notion of working with a partner, to give a task which each child can do fairly easily, so that only the social aspect of the task requires attention (Jordan and Powell, 1995). Once a pupil is used to working with a partner, then the task requirements can become more challenging. Moving from partnered work to small group, large group and whole-class working is likely to be the most effective progression for the majority.

Pamela Hirsch (2001), an able woman with autism, describes her anxieties when she has to do an activity with another person and illustrates how difficult some everyday events can be. Pamela explains: 'It's scary to have something that concerns me directly, under the control of someone else.' She prefers to be in control so that she determines what happens to her, rather than having to fit into or respond to the needs or demands of others. If this feeling is shared by others, it is not surprising that working in a group is particularly stressful. The type of activities which appear relatively successful for group work are music and movement; aerobics; cookery; board games; PE activities; art and craft; action songs; playing and sharing musical instruments; and structured communication activities. Figure 6.2 suggests some of the questions to consider when setting up a group activity.

- *What information about the pupil needs to be taken into account?*
- *What is the nature of the task and its demands for each pupil?*
- *What will be the adult–pupil ratio?*
- *Which other pupils will be in the group?*
- *What are the likely support needs of others in the group?*
- *Which adults will be working in the group?*
- *What might their different roles be?*
- *Has the role of the adults been discussed in advance of the activity?*
- *What is the best physical space and setting for the activity?*
- *What are the objectives of the session for each of the pupils in the group?*
- *Are the instructions to the pupil clear?*
- *How will the beginning and end of the group activities be marked?*

Figure 6.2   Questions to consider on group working

Social skills groups

A number of professionals from psychology, speech therapy and education have created groups to teach social skills (e.g. Mesibov, 1984; Howlin and Yates, 1999). Some groups have been composed solely of those with ASDs and others have had mixed groups, sometimes including the siblings of the children with ASDs (e.g. Howell, 2001). There has been little published on the logistics, content and effectiveness of social skills groups for either children or adults with ASDs. Given what is known about ASDs, such groups might be expected to have limited benefit, as skills are discussed and rehearsed out of the natural context. Evidence suggests that individuals do not easily make links between the work they do in their social skills groups and the real setting (Ozonoff and Miller, 1995). Groups which contain only those with ASDs might offer some reassurance to the participants that there are others who have similar difficulties, but a potential disadvantage is the lack of good role models. Strategies which address social skills as and when situations arise would seem to have more to offer, but more research is required on how best to develop social understanding.

Circle of Friends

There is some excellent work currently in developing Circles of Friends, where the teacher, usually supported by an outside professional, or other member of staff with experience of the intervention, creates a group of peers who befriend and support the child during work and play activities. The group starts off by engineering interactions and social contact but the aim is that these will develop into more natural friendships and there is evidence that this does occur for some children (Taylor, 1997). Those who developed the approach, which is not specifically for children with ASDs, argue that individuals with a disability often have few social contacts outside their immediate family and paid professionals. It is important to establish whether the child would like to develop a Circle of Friends and that their permission is obtained. Ways of describing the strategy to the child and getting his/her opinion will vary with the child's understanding and ability to express his/her views. The process of setting up a Circle has been described in a number of publications (e.g. Taylor, 1997; Whitaker *et al.*, 1998; Essex LEA, 1999). Other details of this strategy are given in Chapter 4.

In establishing a Circle of Friends, an initial discussion is held with the whole class. This discussion is best facilitated by a person who does not teach the class. This could be the SENCO or the Head of year or a visiting professional. The classteacher is then free to observe and take notes. The focus child is generally not present during this discussion, but has given permission for this to occur and the facilitator makes it clear to the class that the focus child knows the discussion is happening. There are just two ground rules. One is that everyone's ideas are respected, and the second is that what is discussed is confidential to the group. The class are then asked to describe situations which go well for them and the focus child, and then to describe situations where things are difficult. The facilitator asks the children to think about the feelings they have had when they have felt excluded from a situation or had no friends and s/he lists these feelings on a flip chart. The children are then asked what they do when they have these feelings. The responses of children of all ages (and adults), to these two key questions, are very similar and seem universal (e.g. upset, angry, sad). One or two children might then make the link and ask, 'Is that why N does . . . ?' If not, the facilitator might suggest this to the class.

The facilitator then asks the class for ideas on how they might improve the situation. Ideas suggested might include 'to sit next to N; play with N at breaktime; go to lunch with N; be N's partner in Science'. The class is given the feeling that the whole class can work together on this and that it's not just the focus child's problem. At the end of the class discussion, the facilitator asks for volunteers to create a Circle of Friends for the child. At a later point, staff decide which of these volunteers will form the Circle. They will select some children who are vulnerable and some who have high status or good social skills, choosing between six and eight children in all.

The Circle then meets with the classteacher and the focus child and feeds back all the positive things about the child. The volunteers explain why they would like to be in the Circle. They discuss ways in which the focus child would like to be included in their activities. Often in schools, adults are employed to help children, when in fact many of the tasks could be effectively and more naturally carried out by other pupils (e.g. putting on a coat; explaining a task; observing or playing with the child at breaktime). The Circle meets weekly to discuss progress and strategies, and continues for as long as it is felt useful, which may be for half a term, a whole term or a whole school year. The facilitator needs to be very skilled, and care needs to be taken that Circle meetings are not spent feeding back negative comments to the focus child. When and how the Circle ends should be carefully planned and agreed. The Circle can be reinstated if the need arises in the future or on transfer to a new class or school.

There have been positive reports on the effects of Circles of Friends (Taylor, 1997; Whitaker et al., 1998). Pupils who had expressed negative feelings towards the child have changed their attitudes and become a friend of the child. Parents of the focus child have found they now have a group of children (the Circle) that they can invite to play with their child. Some pupils have given advice to the focus child on what to wear and which magazines to look at. Other pupils have partnered the focus child in activities and this has led to others, who were not in the Circle, to volunteer to work with the focus child. The Circle can also form a protective barrier between the child and other pupils who, in the past, might have provoked the focus child or set them up to do something inappropriate. In a sense, it increases the number of people 'looking out' for the child.

Creating time and space for the pupil to be alone

In non-directed time, there are differences in the extent to which staff structure sessions and direct the pupils. It is important that a pupil has some completely adult-free time to relax and engage in his/her preferred activity. Those with ASDs have said how important it is to have time alone. Constantly trying to fit into and respond appropriately to others' demands is very effortful and anxiety-provoking. At breaktimes, it is likely to help if there is play or leisure equipment available, as many pupils enjoy climbing or bikes, and apparatus provides a focus. Tarmac alone can be very difficult. In some schools, staff shorten the amount of time spent outdoors and arrange supervised indoor activities. Some pupils with ASDs, though, will like the space afforded outdoors and will benefit from periods outside to enjoy this. In many schools with a unit or resource for pupils with ASDs, a room or base is provided to which pupils can go to relax at planned times or in times of crisis (Barratt and Thomas, 1999; Hesmondhalgh and Breakey, 2001). Within a classroom, providing a quiet area which is screened or a play tent for younger children can be very useful.

Deciding on what to do in the absence of any clues is difficult for a pupil with an ASD. It is therefore helpful when the pupil is given a fixed choice of activities or if other pupils play with the pupil. Some schools have set up a buddy system where volunteers, who are older or the same age, stay with the pupil during play times and engage him/her in activities. The buddies can be involved in some class activities too, such as PE, where having a partner is useful or in helping the pupil to get to the right place and on time. It is useful to have a group of buddies, all of whom get to know and understand the pupil. They can then share the buddy work and absences are covered. Volunteers can work in pairs and rotate every one or two days and meet with staff to discuss ideas and problem-solve.

Summary

• Many agencies and professionals are likely to be involved with pupils with ASDs. It is important to develop good communication systems and agree procedures to give a consistent and continuous service.

- Parents have a great deal of valuable information on their child and effective ways of obtaining this information need to be developed.
- Staff can give strategies to parents on developing communication, social understanding and managing behaviour and a variety of ways of sharing ideas with parents need to be explored.
- Support for the family outside of school hours needs to be extended and developed.
- Sharing information on ASDs and responsibility for pupils between staff is important.
- A consideration of how staff within a school are trained in ASDs is necessary prior to the pupil's placement and on an ongoing basis.
- Given that the staffing ratio for some pupils with ASDs allows for individual teaching sessions, it is important these are planned and work effectively.
- Pupils with ASDs need to be taught the potential value of friendship, so they can make informed choices as to whether to work and play alone or with others.
- Staff need to be social engineers to develop relationships between pupils.
- Pupils with ASDs need time to be alone.
- An assessment of the social networks within a class can be made as a basis for intervention.
- Schools need to have effective anti-bullying procedures.

CHAPTER 7

Life beyond school

Introduction

Children without ASDs can make the necessary adjustments to their skills and understandings gradually, as they pass from childhood to adolescence and into adulthood. Individuals with ASDs, though, find it hard to understand the need to change previously learned behaviours, so it is advisable, where possible, to teach them the skills which are appropriate in later life from the start. Important areas include self-care, vocational skills, leisure skills and understanding social relationships, including sexuality and assertiveness. Lacking skills in these areas will make the individual dependent on others and is likely to lead to difficulties in gaining employment and make the person vulnerable to exploitation and abuse. Currently, there is far less specific literature on strategies and support systems for adolescents and adults with ASDs than there is on those for children, but the literature is growing. Two important and useful texts have been written by Howlin (1997) and Morgan (ed.) (1996) respectively. Hesmondhalgh and Breakey (2001) have also recently produced a book on the needs of secondary-aged pupils with ASDs which gives guidance on making links with colleges and employers and the transition to these. Accounts written by adults with ASDs are a very important and useful addition to this literature.

In the latter years of schooling, decisions need to be made on future provision, and work is geared to preparing the individual for that. Currently, situations arise where future placement is uncertain and decisions on where the pupils move on to are not made until very late. Preparing the student, parents and receiving staff and others for the transfer can then be hurried and inadequate. The TEACCH programme (Schopler and Mesibov, 1995) which was developed in North Carolina in the USA, recognises that many individuals with ASDs require lifelong support and so services continue seamlessly from childhood into adulthood. In the UK, there is often a break in services as the main responsibility and source of funding transfers from education to social services and health authorities, and, in some cases, support for the individual ceases when they leave school. Staff working with pupils in their last two years at school require a good knowledge of options and services for pupils when they leave school. Work is then needed to transfer information and knowledge to future staff about ASDs and about the particular student concerned.

Leaving school and being expected to make choices and function much more independently in the world can highlight the difficulties of young people with ASDs, who may have managed quite well within the structure and support of education and home. In addition to continuing education, the needs of the student in relation to employment, housing, social and sexual relationships and mental health have to be considered. Before discussing these areas, it is important to mention that there are a significant number of adults with ASDs who have not been diagnosed or who have been misdiagnosed with other conditions. All those who work with children and adolescents need to be aware of this and understand the implications of late diagnosis and misdiagnosis.

Late or missed diagnoses

Some individuals with ASDs reach adulthood without receiving a diagnosis. They can be classified into four different groups, as follows:

- those adults with an undiagnosed ASD who are successful and who do not require services over and above those which other people might access as adults;
- those adults with an undiagnosed ASD who struggle to manage their personal or professional lives;
- those adults with an undiagnosed ASD who have been misdiagnosed as having a mental illness such as schizophrenia or obsessive compulsive disorder;
- those adults with an undiagnosed ASD who also have other difficulties.

There are currently many adults with ASDs who have not been recognised. Some individuals might be having their needs met effectively, but many more will have unmet needs and experience problems because employers, carers or staff misunderstand their behaviour and intentions. It is therefore important for staff in schools to help to ensure that those who would benefit from a diagnosis are identified.

Transition reviews and careers advice

In Year 9, a transition plan will be drawn up for pupils with a Statement of SEN, often during the annual review meeting. This plan identifies the pupil's aims and ambitions, the areas to address during the remainder of his/her time at school, the options available when s/he leaves school and the support s/he is likely to require. Parents, the pupil and key staff attend and representatives from social services, health and a careers officer or adviser from the recently established Connexions service are invited. The Connexions service was introduced on a phased basis in April 2001 and, amongst other services, incorporates the work of the Careers Service. Each young person between the ages of 13 to 19 will have a personal adviser and, for those with special needs, this service will be more intensive and can continue until the age of 25. The adviser will provide support and guidance and negotiate on behalf of the student. Additional assessments on their educational and training needs can be arranged between the ages of 16 and 25, if necessary. Students with ASDs are likely to require specialist careers advice and additional support in FE and HE. Even those who have achieved good examination results will usually require considerable support to access, participate and achieve in the less structured setting of a college or university environment. When seeking and gaining employment, they are likely to need, and benefit from, the specific support of job coaches.

At the age of 18, the responsibility for the young person will usually transfer from children's services to adult services within the social services department. It is the responsibility of social services to ascertain whether the individual should be considered as disabled and also to assess whether the person needs support from social services. Ideally, a member of the social services team should attend the last school review, but this is often not possible because of workloads. In addition to assessing the need for support provided by social services, the young person's need for services in relation to education, vocational training, employment, housing and health is ascertained.

Further and higher education

The range of educational provision for pupils with ASDs when they leave school includes further education colleges, higher education institutes or colleges which specialise in meeting the needs of students with ASDs. Some pupils may leave school at the age of 16, but others will stay on until they are 18 or 19. Where the pupil remains at school, they may take part in a school–college link course which can be available to the pupil from the age of 14 and involves part-time college attendance. Based on ideas from the TEACCH programme (Schopler and Mesibov, 1995), centres in the UK were established by the NAS, for the Life Education of Autistic People (LEAP), to provide FE for students with ASDs. Other ordinary FE colleges have made specific provision for students with ASDs (Morgan *et al.*, 1996) and there are one or two specialist FE colleges, some of which are residential, that have been specifically established for this group (Moxon and Gates, 2001).

Some students will attend college or university on a daily basis from their parents' home; others will live at the college or university. With the increased awareness and recognition of ASDs, a greater number of students are being identified within HE and FE. There are still many students, though, who are undiagnosed. Their specific needs may not be identified and some students have been excluded or have decided to stop attending.

Over recent years some FE colleges have been working to enhance provision for this group, often in conjunction with the local autistic society. Students often require help with the non-academic components of life at college and university (e.g. the social times, accessing leisure facilities and canteens, travel, organisation and planning). They also require particular advice on courses to follow and careers after college. Some students have had supporters who are funded to help with aspects of life they find difficult. Others remain living at home in order to receive support from their families. Most FE colleges offer a wide range of courses from part-time to full-time, some of which lead to higher level qualifications and others of which are vocational courses leading to specific types of employment. Some of the courses are specifically designed for those with special educational needs. Every college has a Disability Statement which explains the arrangements for supporting students with learning difficulties and most colleges have at least one member of staff who is responsible for students with special needs.

Preparing a student for a place at an FE college involves choosing an appropriate course, a suitable college, completing the application form and preparing for interview. All these stages will take time. Some staff may role-play the interview situation, video this and feed it back to the student and, in some cases, a member of staff or the pupil's parent will attend the interview (Hesmondhalgh and Breakey, 2001). The time between leaving school and starting at an FE college can be difficult for a student. They lose their identity and the routine associated with school and they have not yet become a college student. Many school staff will work hard to lessen the effects of this 'limbo' state by preparing the student for the transition, making visits to the college and giving them tangible information about the teaching rooms, the staff and the leisure and canteen facilities (Hesmondhalgh and Breakey, 2001).

ESPA (European Services for People with Autism) in the north-east of England works with over 150 adults with ASDs and runs a specialist residential FE college with a 24-hour curriculum (Moxon and Gates, 2001). College terms are extended to 43 weeks to support students and their families. FE funding pays for only 38 weeks and so the social services and health departments provide the extra money needed. Most students at the college also spend part of their time at local sector FE colleges. A range of professionals is available to support the needs of the students, as required, including a psychologist, psychiatrist, speech and language therapist, community psychiatric nurses, GPs, dentists, dieticians and occupational therapists.

Potential difficulties within the FE environment

Morgan *et al.* (1996) listed the features of the typical FE environment which might present problems to many students with ASDs. These included:

- the content of the curriculum, particularly if skills are taught out of context
- spoken language is often the main teaching method
- the teaching environment might be large and noisy
- lack of structure out of lecture times (e.g. breaks; meals; travel)
- lack of staff understanding about ASDs
- lack of peer group understanding of ASDs
- induction period often too short.

Key features of an effective FE placement

Hesmondhalgh and Breakey (2001) see the following as key features in making an FE placement work:

- transition from school is carefully planned using maps, photos, videos and rehearsing, 'what to do if . . .'
- detailed discussions with parents
- the placement is supported by staff who have knowledge of ASDs
- FE staff are given written information on the student and on how to access specialist support
- targets are set for the student with planned review dates.

Higher education

It is only very recently that the needs of students with ASDs in higher education have been recognised and there is still much work to do in terms of raising awareness amongst staff and meeting the students' needs effectively. Before going to university, students need help in deciding which courses to study, which universities to apply to and how to complete the forms. Once at the university, it is the social demands rather than the academic requirements which are likely to present the challenge. For many it will be easier to attend a university close to home so that they can continue to receive support from their family. All universities have a student support team responsible for those with a disability, when the disability is declared by the student. An assessment of the likely needs of the student is then undertaken before the course starts, so that needs can be discussed and resources arranged. Some students choose not to share the fact they have an ASD with the university. Each student needs advice on the relative merits of giving this information to tutors.

Clare Sainsbury (2000) found that in some respects she had fewer problems at university than she did at school, as other students were more tolerant of difference. Wendy Lawson (1998), an adult with Asperger syndrome, gives advice on the type of support that might be required by students in a university or college setting, based on her own experiences. She suggests that the individual should:

- find an autism-friendly person within the university disability section
- find a buddy to act as a guide through the university systems and facilities
- inform their personal tutor of their specific needs
- ask their personal tutor to disseminate information to colleagues.

Particular difficulties which Wendy Lawson encountered, as a mature student, included dealing with locked doors; facing crowded places; travelling in lifts because of the close physical proximity of others; the system for exchanging the sheets; operating the laundry machines; using the swimming pool; finding books in the library; and responding to fire alarm practice. Increasing the awareness of university tutors about ASDs to help them to recognise students with autism and Asperger syndrome would be useful so that they can act as advocates to ensure appropriate support is provided.

Employment

Over the last few years, it has been recognised that providing employment for adults with ASDs at all levels of ability is a basic human right. The European Charter for autism states that: 'People with autism should share the same rights and privileges enjoyed by all of the European population, where such are appropriate and in the best interests of the person with autism' (Autism-Europe, 1992, p. 1).

Supported employment schemes have emerged in the UK, although most individuals in these schemes, to date, have been those who are more able and those with mild or moderate autism. In the USA though, Datlow Smith *et al.* (1995) describe supported employment over 15 years, with more than 70 adults with ASDs, most of whom had severe learning difficulties. Their book serves to encourage others to find employment for individuals who have seemed unemployable and unsupportable. They found that it was crucial to provide supervision and feedback for as long as it was required.

In 1994, the NAS set up a supported employment scheme known as Prospects, which offers support to individuals, their employers and employees in the London and Glasgow areas. In 1999, there were 41 organisations using Prospects in retail, travel, banking, health trusts and manufacturing. Spence and Penney (1991), two support workers with Prospects, have written about the strategies used to support the employment process. In the West Midlands, the regional autistic society has set up a similar employment scheme called Aspire. Research into the outcomes of the Prospects employment scheme in the UK, in which 30 adults with ASDs took part, and which compared their success to 20 similar adults who were not supported, showed that more of the supported group found work, that the levels of job were higher, that they were in work for longer and that they had higher levels of pay. There were 13 different employers, mainly large, multinational companies. Although the initial costs of the scheme were high, these decreased significantly over time, as the adults required decreasing levels of support. One of the most time-consuming parts of the scheme was finding the right employment.

In their work with secondary-aged pupils with ASDs, Hesmondhalgh and Breakey (2001) have set up work experience and feel it is vital to start working towards work as early as possible. Staff felt depressed initially, as very few employers responded to their requests for placement. Responses have increased as the scheme has met with success. Since starting the scheme, many pupils have done extremely well and their self-esteem has increased enormously. The staff within the secondary school resource argue that funding from central government should be made available, as a matter of course, to provide support workers. Training and Enterprise Councils (TECS) are now responsible for arranging work-related training for young people and adults in local colleges or private training organisations. People up to the age of 25 can be considered for training and all students work towards a National Vocational Qualification (NVQ).

Students at school or college need a thorough vocational assessment to ascertain the type of employment to which they are most suited. Areas to assess include:

- work skills (e.g. personal appearance, punctuality, transport requirements)
- communication skills
- social skills
- response to verbal instructions
- requisite skills for the job
- academic skills (e.g. literacy and numeracy)
- learning style (e.g. by demonstration; physical prompting; written lists)
- vocational preference (e.g. likes and dislikes)
- triggers for problem behaviour.

This list could also be useful prior to the student's attendance at a college. Factors which might lead to problems in the workplace include poor job match, change of personnel, unclear expectations and changing demands and priorities. Mastering the skills required for the job is generally much easier than understanding the 'office politics' and hidden agendas which involve reading social signals and underlying intentions. These skills are much more difficult to teach and finding employment where this is less of an issue can be hard.

Type of employment which best suits those with autistic spectrum disorders

The types of employment which would generally suit individuals with ASDs include those

- with a limited need to communicate with others
- with low sensory stimuli
- with clear targets
- with few daily changes
- which link to a special interest or skill (e.g. paper, lists, visual patterns)
- which require attention to detail.

These include jobs in stock control, library work, maintenance of databases, architecture, computing, accountancy and research. The strengths of those with ASDs, which make them attractive to employers, are their attention to detail, their honesty, their time-keeping, and their good on-task skills. Don Meyer (2001), an adult with Asperger syndrome, has written a guide for others, which advises on the various aspects of seeking and maintaining employment. He also discusses how much information to give to others about the diagnosis and its implications.

Housing

Currently, most diagnosed adults continue to live with their parents or in supported accommodation with others who have learning difficulties or ASDs. Very few such individuals live on their own, and those that do, generally still need frequent advice and support by telephone and visits from relatives, if they are to have a reasonable quality of life. A greater proportion of diagnosed adults could live on their own if there were more schemes to provide the support they required. As yet, there are only a few examples of such support systems (MacLeod, 1999) and these are often called projects, which reflects their temporary and innovative nature, rather than being a permanent part of mainstream services.

The range of accommodation options should include the opportunity to live alone, with staff support, as necessary, as sharing a house with staff and others with learning difficulties can add to their difficulties. The behaviour of staff and other residents may be intrusive and disturb the world that the person with an ASD wants to create and preserve. Ros Blackburn, an able person with an ASD, lives in a flat on her own. She refers to this flat as her 'autism paradise' (Blackburn, 2000), as her time within it, and the environment she creates, is totally under her control, with no intrusion from others, except by invitation. Her ideal would be to have a system of support which she could call on when needed, so that she is not solely dependent on her parents when she needs practical or emotional advice and help.

Supported tenancies allow adults to live in their own homes and can be ideal for those with ASDs. Staff can visit on a regular basis to advise and give support, as necessary. Consistency, calmness, structure, predictability and empathy are all important attributes of the environment and the personal style of staff. Not all adults with ASDs want to live alone, however, nor do they always need to live in settings where all the residents have ASDs. Some adults live successfully with adults with learning difficulties. So, it is important that a range of accommodation is provided for this population. What is crucial is that the staff know the individual has an ASD and that they understand the implications of this.

Social and sexual relationships

Assumptions have been made about the sexual behaviour and needs of those with ASDs. As many individuals with ASDs do not engage easily in social relationships and may not show an interest in forming friendships, some professionals have felt that sex education has not been necessary. Others have taken a moral stance and felt that sexual relationships outside marriage should not be encouraged. However, a study by Van Bourgondien *et al.* (1997) showed that most adults with autism engaged in some form of sexual behaviour, usually masturbation, and some showed sexual interest in other people. Similarly, Haracopos and Pedersen (1994) studied 55 adults with autism aged between 16 to 40 years in a residential setting. They found that 74 per cent of males and 54 per cent of females masturbated, often using objects or materials as a stimulus, rather than images of people. This fits with the view that those with ASDs are usually not people-focused.

Most people without ASDs develop their knowledge and understanding of sexual behaviour through discussions with their peer group and from literature, TV and films. Many individuals with ASDs have limited access to these. In addition, understanding human behaviour and interacting appropriately with others in all social situations is a real challenge for those with ASDs. In the area of intimate, sexual behaviour, teaching an individual what is appropriate and how to respond to others is extremely difficult. Few materials have been developed, as yet, specifically for individuals with ASDs. Specific materials have been developed for those with learning difficulties (Craft, 1987; Eales and Watson, 1994). Downs (1998) discusses the challenges and dilemmas for staff in teaching children with severe and profound learning difficulties about sexuality. There is a need for structured programmes, with clear visual and unambiguous information. Programmes such as *Living your life* (Craft, 1991), for individuals with learning difficulties, often require relatively good interactive and social skills. Hobbs (1999) suggests that the materials needed for those with ASDs should take a less social and less morally oriented approach.

McCarthy (1999) has written a book which focuses solely on the sexual experiences of women with learning disabilities. There is no specific mention, though, of women with ASDs. Her research identified a high incidence of sexual abuse perpetrated by other service-users. Many issues of relevance to school staff and service providers and those engaged in sex education are raised. In particular, McCarthy (1999) recommends that there should be separate sex education sessions for males and females, unless there is value in joint discussions, and an acknowledgement that women can gain pleasure from sex. Staff should also be made aware that women are often abused in their sexual relationships with men, even where consent has been given.

Hesmondhalgh and Breakey (2001) involve the parents of pupils in discussions about the sex education programmes they wish to teach, both prior to the start of the programme and during this work. They use a 'problem page' strategy where the pupils respond to fictitious letters asking for advice on relationships and sexual behaviour. This enables staff to assess the pupils' understanding of sexual behaviour and relationships, and to plan further work. Individuals with ASDs are vulnerable to sexual exploitation and abuse both in the community and within residential settings (Booth and Booth, 1992; Hobbs, 1999). Assertiveness training and creating an awareness of what is OK and not OK in terms of what they do and how they behave towards others, and what others might suggest to them, is also a very important part of sex education.

Tew (1999) argues that individuals with ASDs may behave, unintentionally, in ways which appear to have sexual intent, but which do not. For example, an individual who likes the feel of a certain texture might stroke another person, without realising how this might be interpreted. Such incidents have led to criminal charges being made in some cases. Staff and parents therefore need to analyse behaviour carefully before assuming it is sexually motivated and then teach alternative behaviour. Pamela Maddock (1996), the principal of a school for pupils with ASDs, has produced a useful set of guidelines on the policy and procedures in relation to sexuality for staff in schools for children with ASDs. This gives advice on the law, staff attitudes, the prerequisites for staff giving sex education and the assessment of the needs of individuals.

Mental health

During adolescence and into adulthood, some individuals with ASDs develop mental health disorders. They may become increasingly aware of the differences between themselves and their peers, and relationships with classmates may decline. Kim *et al.* (2000) studied 59 adolescents with high functioning autism (40) and Asperger syndrome (19) in Canada and compared the evidence for psychiatric problems, including mood and anxiety disorders, with a group of 1,751 normally developing individuals. The students with ASDs showed a greater rate of depression and anxiety problems.

Staff can work to maintain the links the individual has with their peers, perhaps by reinstating previous strategies such as Circles of Friends (Whitaker *et al.*, 1998). Offering a specific time during the school week to discuss issues with a member of staff who has knowledge of ASDs can be helpful. Hesmondhalgh and Breakey (2001) ask students to complete a worry recording sheet to state what their worries are, how serious these are and whom they might discuss them with. This gives the students experience in naming their concerns and sharing these with others. For individuals with ASDs who have excellent speech and a high level of ability in some areas, the general public often expects them to perform 'normally', be it on the telephone, having a meal or when discussing work issues. Howlin (2000), in reviewing the outcome for able adults with autism, says that there is often constant pressure to fit in by a society who fails to understand their needs and difficulties. A failure to meet those demands can cause great distress and anxiety and, in some cases, psychiatric breakdown. A mature and able woman with an ASD illustrates these points well in the following comment to Theo Peeters, 'It will be a shock to you to see how convincingly I can be normal – but in being normal I am unconnected with myself' (Peeters, 2000).

The particular needs of able adults with autistic spectrum disorders

The intellectual ability of those who are high functioning or who have Asperger syndrome can mask their difficulties in other areas and so their need for support is not recognised. But, the ability to speak fluently and achieve high grades in certain subjects does not equate to being competent in everyday activities such as cooking, crossing the road or going to a cafe. Some adults can seem fairly able when supported with another person, in tasks such as shopping, using public transport or visiting a new place, but can have major problems when doing these on their own. Some need to attend for medical checks or treatment, but do not do so as they lack the skills required to make the appointment or access the surgery or clinic. A thorough assessment of their life and independence skills and ability to problem-solve in different settings and contexts is required to ensure incorrect assumptions are not made on the basis of partial information. Appropriate support then needs to be offered to enable the person to manage their daily lives and needs in relation to employment, housing, leisure and health.

When the child is in education, parents can feel relatively well supported, but once their child has left school or college, support and services may disappear. Parents become less physically and emotionally able to support their adult sons and daughters and yet they are often expected to be the sole provider of such support. This clearly places a huge burden on parents whose own health is then likely to suffer and who may then require services themselves. In the USA, effective circles of support have been established for adults with disabilities made up of people already known to them (e.g. shopkeepers; leisure centre employees; churchgoers; relatives). The circle meets regularly with the adult concerned, to discuss issues and make and agree plans. The individual is able to contact people in their circle for a chat, or advice, and arrangements can be made to visit shared places of interest. Such circles have been created in the UK for adults with other disabilities as well as ASDs, but these are relatively rare, as yet.

As effective schemes and services to support adults with ASDs in continuing education, employment and leisure are developed, so professionals and voluntary organisations in other areas of the country can use these as models to design more effective services. Providing appropriate support from the outset is likely to reduce the need to provide more expensive services later on, when the individual becomes depressed, unemployed or challenging as a result of services which are inadequate and inappropriate. With increasing knowledge and training, and respect for the perspective and wishes of those with ASDs, the support available is likely to improve, and the lives and well-being of people with ASDs and their families will be enhanced.

Summary

- Staff working with pupils with ASDs need to take a long-term perspective and work on skills needed in adult life during the school years.
- Many adults with ASDs are late to be diagnosed or are not diagnosed at all.
- Transition reviews occur in Year 9 to plan for the pupil's future when they leave school.
- FE colleges are increasing their awareness and developing provision for students with ASDs.
- There are many students in FE and HE with ASDs who are not recognised as such.
- Individuals with ASDs will need support in finding appropriate employment and in learning the skills required to do the job.
- Housing and support schemes needs to be developed and extended to allow adults with ASDs to live on their own, if this is in their interests.
- Sex education and assertiveness programmes are important aspects of the curriculum for all pupils with ASD.
- Some adults with ASDs develop mental health disorders, some as a result of the lack of support available.
- There needs to be greater awareness and more accurate assessment of the needs of able adults with ASDs.

Proforma for tracking the educational provision made for pupils with autistic spectrum disorders

There is currently little long-term data on the educational routes taken by children with ASDs and on what basis decisions are made about provision. Nor is there much information on their outcome as young adults, and the extent to which earlier provision influences this outcome. Such information would be valuable for devising and planning provision for this group of pupils.

Below is a possible proforma which education authorities might use to monitor and track the educational placement of children with ASDs.

Proforma for tracking the educational provision made for pupils with autistic spectrum disorders

The purpose of this form is to collect information on pupils with ASDs when they transfer out of a school or unit. This information will be collated by the education authority to use for planning provision for this group of pupils.

This should be completed by staff in the school/unit which the pupil is leaving during the half term before the child leaves. It should then be sent to a named person within the education authority.

Name of person completing the form: _____

Position within the school: _____ Tel: _____

Date of completion: _____

1   Name of child: _____

2   Date of birth of child: _____

3   Main diagnosis: _____

4   Any additional diagnoses: (e.g. epilepsy; dyslexia; ADHD; dyspraxia)

_____

5   Name of current school: _____

6   Type of school/unit: (please circle)

   a   mainstream   mld   sld   ebd   specific to autism

      other, please specify: _____

   b   EA   independent   other EA

   c   day   residential placement, weekly, termly, 50 weeks a year

7   Date of admission to the school: _____   Age in years: _____

8   Does the child have a Statement/Record of Needs?   YES   NO

   If YES, which year was this first issued: _____

9   Approximate cost of the placement at the school/unit for the pupil during the last financial year (excluding any transport costs):

   £_____ per year   don't know

10   Did the child have an assistant allocated specifically to work with them? YES   NO
    If YES:

   a   for how many hours per week? _____

   b   to offer support in what type of situation? _____

11   Please state briefly why the child is leaving this school/unit

_____

_____

12   Which school/unit is s/he moving on to?

   a   Name of school/unit: _____

   b   Type of school/unit:

      mainstream   mld   sld   ebd   specific to autism

      other, please specify: _____

   c   EA   independent   other EA

   d   day   residential placement, weekly, termly, 50 weeks a year

13   Which factors determined the choice of the next placement and why is it thought suitable for the child?

_____

_____

14 Skills and abilities of the child on leaving your school/unit

Tick all those which apply or write your own description:

Dimension	Skill	Comment
Expressive language skills	mainly uses photos/pictures/symbols	
	mainly uses signs	
	single spoken words; short phrases; full sentences	
Social skills	prefers to be alone	
	wants friends	
	is able to work or play with another child/with children	
Behaviours	less demanding than ordinary peers; more demanding than ordinary peers; very demanding	
Academic skills	Reading accuracy at his/her age level/ below age level/well below age level/ not able to read	
	Reading comprehension at his/her age level/below age level/well below age level/not able to read	
	Can write at his/her age level/below age level/well below age level/not able to write	
Overall intellectual ability	above/average/below average/well below average	

References

ACCAC (2000) *A structure for success: guidance on the National Curriculum and autistic spectrum disorder.* Cardiff: QCAA.

Aird, R. and Lister, J. (1999) 'Enhancing provision for pupils with autism within a school for children with severe learning difficulties', in Jones, G. (ed.) *Good Autism Practice, April 1999.* Birmingham: University of Birmingham.

Aldred, C. *et al.* (2001) 'Multidisciplinary social communication intervention for children with autism and pervasive developmental disorder: the Child's Talk project', *Educational and Child Psychology,* **18**(2), 76–87.

Allen, J. I. (1980) 'Jogging can modify disruptive behaviors', *Teaching Exceptional Children,* **12**, 66–70.

American Psychiatric Association (1994) *Diagnostic and Statistical Manual of Mental Disorders,* Fourth edition – Revised (DSM IV-R). Washington, DC: American Psychiatric Association.

Aston, G. (2000) 'Through the eyes of autism', *Good Autism Practice Journal,* **1**(2), 57–61.

Attwood, T. (1998) *Asperger syndrome: a guide for parents and professionals.* London: Jessica Kingsley.

Attwood, T. (2000) 'Strategies for improving the social integration of children with Asperger syndrome', *Autism,* **4**(1), 85–100.

Attwood, T. *et al.* (1988) 'The understanding and use of interpersonal gestures by autistic and Down's syndrome children', *Journal of Autism and Developmental Disorders,* **18**, 241–57.

Autism-Europe (1992) 'Charter for people with autism', presented at the 4th Autisme Europe Congress, Haag, 10 May, 1992.

Bailey, A. *et al.* (1996) 'Autism: towards an integration of clincal, genetic, neuropsychological and neurobiological perspectives', *Journal of Child Psychology and Psychiatry,* **37**(1), 89–126.

Baillie, R. (2000) 'Care Standards Bill (1999) and Modernising Social Services', *Good Autism Practice Journal,* **1**(2), 28–34.

Baird, G. (2000) 'A screening instrument for autism at 18 months of age: a 6 year follow-up study', *Journal of American Academic Child and Adolescent Psychiatry,* **39**, 694–702.

Baker, A. F. (1983) 'Psychological assessment of autistic children', *Clinical Psychology Review,* **3**, 41–59.

Balfe, P. (2001) 'A study of the induction experiences and the needs of teachers new to autistic spectrum disorders in the Republic of Ireland', *Good Autism Practice Journal*, 2(2), 75–85.

Barber, C. (1996) 'The integration of a very able pupil with Asperger syndrome into a mainstream school', *British Journal of Special Education*, 23, 19–24.

Baron-Cohen, S. (2000) *Understanding others' minds*. Oxford: Oxford University Press.

Baron-Cohen, S. *et al.* (1992) 'Can autism be detected at 18 months? The needle, the haystack and the CHAT', *British Journal of Psychiatry*, 161, 839–43.

Barratt, P. and Thomas, B. (1999) 'The inclusion of students with Asperger syndrome in a mainstream secondary school: a case study', in Jones, G. (ed.) *Good Autism Practice, September 1999*. Birmingham: University of Birmingham.

Bartolo, P. (2001) 'How disciplinary and institutional orientation influences professionals' decision-making about early childhood disability', *Educational and Child Psychology*, 18(2), 88–106.

Beyer, J. and Gammeltoft, L. (1999) *Autism and play*. London: Jessica Kingsley.

Birkin, P. (2000) 'Children with an autistic spectrum disorder and educational visits', *Good Autism Practice Journal*, 1(2), 35–41.

Bishop, D. V. M. (1989a) 'Autism, Asperger's syndrome, semantic pragmatic disorder: where are the boundaries?' *British Journal of Disorders of Communication*, 24, 107–21.

Bishop, D. V. M. (1989b) *Test of Reception of Grammar*. Cambridge: Applied Psychology Unit.

Bishop, D. V. M. (1998) 'Development of the Checklist of Communicative Competence (CCC): a method for assessing qualitative aspects of communicative impairment in children', *Journal of Child Psychology and Psychiatry*, 39(6), 879–91.

Bishop, D. V. M. (1999) *Checklist of Communicative Competence*.

Blackburn, R. (2000) 'Within and without autism', *Good Autism Practice Journal*, 1(1), 2–8.

Bolton, P. *et al.* (1994) 'A case-control family history study of autism', *Journal of Child Psychology and Psychiatry*, 35, 877–900.

Bondy, A. S. and Frost, L. A. (1994) 'The Delaware autistic program', in Harris, S. L. and Handleman, J. S. (eds) *Preschool education programs for children with autism*, Austin, TX: Pro-Ed.

Booth, T. and Booth, W. (1992) 'Practice in sexuality', in Craft, A. and Harris, J. (eds) 'Sexuality: meeting the needs of people with learning disabilities', *Mental Handicap*, 20(2), ??.

Bristol, M. M. *et al.* (1996) 'State of the science in autism: report to the National Institute of Health', *Journal of Autism and Developmental Disorders*, 26, 121–54.

Burlton, G. (1999) 'Analysing and managing the behaviour of an adult with autism who presents a challenge to an organisation', in Jones, G. (ed.) *Good Autism Practice, April 1999*. Birmingham: University of Birmingham.

Campbell, K and Gregory, V. (2000) *Someone I know has autism*, Hertford: Hertfordshire County Council.

Carpenter, B. *et al.* (2001) 'An evaluation of SIECCA: an intensive programme of education and care for students with profound autistic spectrum disorders', *Good Autism Practice Journal*, 2(1), 52–66.

Carrington, S. and Graham, L. (2001) 'Perceptions of school by two teenage boys with Asperger syndrome and their mothers: a qualitative study', *Autism*, 5(1), 37–48.

Carter, A. S. *et al.* (1998) 'The Vineland Adaptive Behavior Scale: supplementary norms for individuals with autism', *Journal of Autism and Developmental Disorders*, 28, 287–302.

Cass, H. (1998) 'Autism and visual impairment: current questions and research', *Autism*, 2(2), 117–38.

Christie, P. and Chandler, S. (2002) 'A diagnostic and intervention package for young children with autistic spectrum disorders', *Good Autism Practice Journal*, 3(1), 2–13.

Christie, P. and Fidler, R. (2001) 'A continuum of provision for a continuum of need: opportunities for mainstream integration and inclusion provided by a specialist school for children with autism', *Good Autism Practice Journal*, 2(1), 35–44.

Christie, P. *et al.* (1992) 'An interactive approach to language and communication for non-speaking children', in D. Lane and A. Miller (eds) *Child and adolescent therapy*. Milton Keynes: Open University Press.

Clements, J. and Zarkowska, E. (2000) *Behavioural concerns and autistic spectrum disorders*. London: Jessica Kingsley.

Clethero, S. (2000) 'An exploration into creativity: music and drama groups for adults with an autistic spectrum disorder', *Good Autism Practice Journal*, 1(2), 2–7.

Clethero, S. (2001) 'An exploration of creativity', *Good Autism Practice Journal*, 2(1).

Collins, M. *et al.* (1995) *Common ground: report on a visit to the Boston Higashi school*. London: NAS.

Connor, M. (1998) 'A review of behavioural early intervention programmes for children with autism', *Educational Psychology in Practice*, 14(2), 109–17.

Craft, A. (1987) *Mental handicap and sexuality*. Tunbridge Wells: Costello.

Craft, A. (1991) *Living your life*. London: LDA.

Cumine, V. *et al.* (2000) *Autism in the early years: a practical guide*. London: David Fulton Publishers.

Dale, N. (1996) *Working with families of children with special needs*. London: Routledge.

Datlow Smith, M. D. *et al.* (1995) *A guide to successful employment for individuals with autism*. Baltimore, MD: Brookes.

Davies, J. (1995a) *Children with autism: a booklet for brothers and sisters*, see 1995b below for publication details.

Davies, J. (1995b) *Children with Asperger syndrome: a booklet for brothers and sisters*, this publication and 1995a above are available from the Early Years Centre, 272 Longdale Lane, Ravenshead, Nottinghamshire, NG15 9AH.

Dawson, G. and Osterling, J. (1997) 'Early intervention in autism', in Guralnick, M. (ed.) *The effectiveness of early intervention*. Baltimore: Brookes.

DeMyer, M. K. *et al.* (1973) 'Prognosis in autism: a follow-up study', *Journal of Autism and Childhood Schizophrenia*, 3, 199–246.

Department for Education (1994) *Code of Practice*. London: HMSO.

Department for Education and Employment (1998a) *The National Literacy Strategy*. London: DfEE.

Department for Education and Employment (1998b) *Meeting special educational needs: a programme for action*. London: DfEE.

Department for Education and Skills (2001) *Special Educational Needs Code of Practice*. London: DfES.

Department for Education and Skills (in press) *Good practice guidance in autistic spectrum disorders*. London: DfES.

Department of Health (2001*) Valuing people*, London: HMSO.

Dewart, H. and Summers, S. (1988) *The pragmatics profile of early communication skills*, Windsor: NFER-Nelson.

DiLavore, P. C. *et al.* (1995) 'The prelinguistic autism diagnostic observation schedule', *Journal of Autism and Developmental Disorders*, **25**(4), 355–79.

Downs, C. (1998) 'Sexuality: challenges and dilemmas', in Lacey, P. and Ouvry, C. (eds) *People with profound and multiple learning disabilities*, London: David Fulton Publishers.

Drake, S. (2001) 'The challenges involved in implementing the National Literacy Strategy to children with an autistic spectrum disorder and additional learning difficulties in Reception and Key Stage 1 and how these might be addressed', *Good Autism Practice Journal*, **2**(2), 30–47.

Dunn, L. M. *et al.* (1982) *British Picture Vocabulary Scale*. London: NFER-Nelson.

Eales, J. and Watson, J. (1994) 'Health education and special educational needs: Scottish concerns and curriculum framework', *Health Education Journal*, **53**(1), 81–91.

Edwards *et al.* (1997) *Reynell Developmental Language Scales III*. Slough: NFER-Nelson.

Ehlers, S. and Gillberg, C. (1993) 'The epidemiology of Asperger syndrome: a total population study', *Journal of Child Psychology and Psychiatry*, **34**(8), 1327–50.

English, A. (1999) 'Working together: a multi-agency approach to supporting parents of children with autism', in G. Jones (ed.) *Good Autism Practice, April 1999*. Birmingham: University of Birmingham.

Essex LEA (1999) *Circle of Friends (video and pack)* Available from Essex County Council Learning Services, PO Box 47, County Hall, Chelmsford, CM2 6WN; cost £50–00.

Evans, G. (1997) 'The development of the outdoor education programme at Storm House school', in Powell, S. and Jordan, R. (eds) *Autism and learning*. London: David Fulton Publishers.

Evans, J. *et al.* (2001) *Making a difference: early interventions for children with autistic spectrum disorders: LGA research Report 22*. Slough: NFER-Nelson.

Fombonne, E. (1999) 'The epidemiology of autism: a review', *Psychological Medicine*, **29**, 769–86.

Freeman, B. J. (1997) 'Guidelines for evaluating intervention programs for children with autism', *Journal of Autism and Developmental Disorders*, **27**, 641–52.

Freeman, B. J. *et al.* (1991) 'The stability of cognitive and behavioral parameters in autism: a twelve year prospective study', *Journal of American Academy of Child and Adolescent Psychiatry*, **30**, 479–82.

Frith, U. (1989) *Autism: Explaining the enigma*. Oxford: Blackwell.

Gabler-Halle, J. W. *et al.* (1993) 'The effects of aerobic exercise on psychological and behavioral variables of individuals with developmental disabilities: a critical review', *Research in Developmental Disabilities*, **14**, 359–86.

Gagnon, L. *et al.* (1997) 'Questioning the validity of the semantic pragmatic syndrome diagnosis', *Autism*, **1**(1), 37–55.

Gerland, G. (1997) *A real person*. London: Souvenir Press.

Gillberg, C. (2000) 'An overview of the biology of autism'. Paper presented at the Autism Europe Congress, Glasgow.

Gillberg, C. and Steffenburg, S. (1987) 'Outcome and prognostic factors in infantile autism and similar conditions: a population-based study of 46 cases followed through puberty', *Journal of Autism and Developmental Disorders*, 17, 72–288.

Gillberg, C. *et al.* (1991) 'Autism – epidemiology: is autism more common now than it was 10 years ago?' *British Journal of Psychiatry*, 158, 403–9.

Gillberg, C. *et al.* (2001) 'The Asperger syndrome (and high-functioning autism) Diagnostic Interview (ASDI): a preliminary study of a new structured clinical interview', *Autism*, 5(1), 57–66.

Girolametto, L. E. and Greenberg, J. (1986) 'Developing dialogue skills: the Hanen early language parent program', *Seminars in speech and language*, 7(4), 367–82.

Gould, J. *et al.* (1991) *The Higashi experience*. London: National Autistic Society.

Grandin, T. (1995) *Thinking in pictures and other reports from my life with autism*. New York: Doubleday.

Grandin, T. and Scariano, M. M. (1986) *Emergence labeled autistic*. Novato, CA: Arena Press.

Gray, C. (1994a) *The social story book*. Arlington, TX: Future Horizons.

Gray C. (1994b) *Comic strip conversations*. Arlington, TX: Future Horizons.

Gray, C. (2000) 'From both sides now: how to teach social understanding'. Paper presented at the Autism Europe Congress, Glasgow.

Green, G. (1996) 'Early behavioral intervention in autism: what does research tell us?' in Maurice, C. (ed.) *Behavioral intervention for young children with autism*. Austin, TX: Pro-Ed.

Greenspan, S. and Wieder, S. (1999) 'A functional developmental approach to autism spectrum disorders', *Journal of the Association of Persons with Severe Handicaps*, 24, 147–161.

Gringras, P. (2000) 'Practical paediatric psychopharmacological prescribing in autism: the potential and the pitfalls', *Autism*, 4(3), 229–47.

Gringras, P. and McNicholas, F. (1999) 'Developing rational protocols for paediatric psychopharmacological prescribing', *Child: Care, Health and Development*, 25, 223–33.

Grove, N. and Walker, M. (1990) *The Makaton vocabulary: using manual signs and graphic symbols to develop interpersonal communication*. AAC, 15–28.

Hadwin, J. and Hutley, G. (1998) 'Detecting features of autism in children with severe learning difficulties', *Autism*, 2(3), 269–80.

Hadwin, J. *et al.* (1997) 'Does teaching theory of mind have an effect on social communication in children with autism?' *Journal of Autism and Developmental Disorders*, 27, 519–39.

Hale, A. (1998) *My world is not your world*. Ingatestone: Archimedes Press.

Happe, F. (1999) 'Autism: cognitive deficit or cognitive style?' *Trends in Cognitive Science*, 3, 216–22.

Haracopos, D. and Pedersen, L. (1994) 'Sexuality and autism', in Shattock, P. and Linfoot, G. (eds) *Autism on the agenda*, Sunderland: Autism Research Unit.

Harris, S. L. (1994) *Siblings of children with autism*. Bethesda, MD:Woodbine House.

Harris, S. L. and Handleman, J. S. (1994) *Preschool education programs for children with autism*, Austin, TX: Pro-Ed.

Helps, S. *et al.* (1999) 'Autism: the teacher's view', *Autism*, **3**(3), 287–98.

Hesmondhalgh, M. and Breakey, C. (2001) *Access and inclusion for children with autistic spectrum disorders*, London: Jessica Kingsley.

Hewett, D. and Nind, M. (1998) *Interaction in action*. London: David Fulton Publishers.

Hirsch, P. (2001) 'A day in the life of . . . ', *Good Autism Practice Journal*, **2**(1), 7–11.

Hobbs, C. (1999) 'Sex education for adolescents with autism', in Jones, G. (ed.) *Good Autism Practice, April 1999*. Birmingham: University of Birmingham.

Howell, L. (2001) 'Integrative play in children with autism and Asperger syndrome', in Richer, J. and Coates, S. (eds) *Autism: the search for coherence*. London: Jessica Kingsley.

Howlin, P. (1997) *Autism: preparing for adulthood*. London: Routledge.

Howlin, P. (1998a) *Children with Autism and Asperger Syndrome*. London: Wiley.

Howlin, P. (1998b) 'Practitioner review: psychological and educational treatment for autism', *Journal of Child Psychology and Psychiatry*, **39**(3), 307–22.

Howlin, P. (2000) 'Outcome in adult life for more able individuals with autism or Asperger syndrome', *Autism*, **4**(1), 63–83.

Howlin, P. *et al.* (1998) *Teaching children with autism to mind-read: a practical guide for teachers and parents*. London: Wiley.

Howlin, P. and Moore, A. (1997) 'Diagnosis in autism – a survey of 1200 patients', *Autism*, **1**(2), 135–62.

Howlin, P. and Rutter, M. (1987) *Treatment of autistic children*. London: Wiley.

Howlin, P. and Yates, P. (1999) 'The potential effectiveness of social skills groups for adults with autism', *Autism*, **3**(3), 299–307.

Hyde, C. *et al.* (2001) 'Coding of active sociability in preschoolers with autism', in J. Richer and S. Coates (eds) *Autism: the search for coherence*. London: Jessica Kingsley.

Inchley, M. (2001) 'An analysis of the literacy hour for a child with an asd in a school for children with moderate learning difficulties', *Good Autism Practice Journal*, **2**(2), 48–58.

Jarbrink, K. and Knapp, M. (2001) 'The economic impact of autism in Britain', *Autism*, **5**(1), 7–22.

Jarrold, C. *et al.* (1993) 'Symbolic play in autism: a review', *Journal of Autism and Developmental Disorders*, **23**(2), 281–8.

Jenkinson, J. (1997) *Mainstream or special*. London: Routledge.

Jones, G. (2001) 'Giving the diagnosis to the young person with Asperger syndrome or high functioning autism', *Good Autism Practice Journal*, **2**(2), 65–74.

Jones, G. and Newson, E. (1992a) 'Policy and provision for children and adults with autism in England and Wales: Report 1'. Unpublished report. Available from Glenys Jones, School of Education, University of Birmingham, Birmingham, B15 2TT.

Jones, G. and Newson, E. (1992b) 'Educational provision for children with autism in England and Wales: Report 2'. Unpublished report. Available from Glenys Jones, School of Education, University of Birmingham.

Jones, G. *et al.* (1995) 'A descriptive and comparative study of interventions for children with autism: summary report'. Unpublished report. Available from Glenys Jones, School of Education, University of Birmingham, Birmingham, B15 2TT.

Jones, J. (2000) 'Passports to children with autism', *Good Autism Practice Journal*, 1(1), 56–65.

Jordan, R. (1999) 'Evaluating practice: problems and possibilities', *Autism: the International Journal of Research and Practice*, 3(4), 411–34.

Jordan, R. (2001) *Autism with severe learning difficulties.* London: Souvenir Press.

Jordan, R. and Jones, G. (1996) *Educational provision for children with autism in Scotland: Final Report of a research project for the SOEID.* Birmingham: School of Education, University of Birmingham.

Jordan, R. and Jones, G. (1999a) *Meeting the needs of children with autistic spectrum disorders.* London: David Fulton Publishers.

Jordan, R. and Jones, G. (1999b) 'Review of research into educational interventions for children with autism', *Autism*, 3(1), 101–10.

Jordan, R. and Peeters, T. (1999) 'What makes a good practitioner in the field of autism?' in Jones, G. (ed.) *Good Autism Practice.* Birmingham: Birmingham University.

Jordan, R. and Powell, S. (1995) *Understanding and teaching children with autism,* Chichester: Wiley.

Jordan, R. and Powell, S. (1996) 'Therapist drift: identifying a new phenomenon in evaluating therapeutic approaches', in Linfoot, G. and Shattock, P. (eds) *Therapeutic intervention in autism.* Sunderland: Autism Research Unit.

Jordan, R. *et al.* (1998) *Educational interventions for children with autism: a literature review of recent and current research, Report 77.* Sudbury: DfEE. Available for £4–95 from DfEE Publications, PO Box 5050, Sherwood Park, Annesley, Nottingham, NG15 0DJ.

Jordan, R. *et al.* (1999) 'Making special schools "specialist": a case study of the provision for pupils with autism in a school for children with severe learning difficulties', in Jones, G. (ed.) *Good Autism Practice.* Birmingham: Birmingham University.

Kaufman, B. N. (1976) *To love is to be happy with.* London: Souvenir Press.

Kaufman, B. N. (1994) *Son rise: the miracle continues.* California: H. J. Kramer.

Kent, L. *et al.* (1998) 'Autism in Down's syndrome: three case reports', *Autism*, 2(3), 259–67.

Kiernan, C. C. and Reid, B. (1987) *Preverbal communication schedule,* Slough: NFER-Nelson.

Kim, J. A. *et al.* (2000) 'The prevalence of anxiety and mood problems among children with autism and Asperger syndrome', *Autism*, 4(2), 117–32.

Kitahara, K. (1984) *Daily Life Therapy: a method of educating autistic children, Vols. 1, 2 and 3.* Boston, MA: Nimrod Press.

Knivsberg, A. M. *et al.* (1995) 'Autistic syndromes and diet', *Scandinavian Journal of Educational Research*, 39, 223–226.

Knott, F. *et al.* (1995) 'Sibling interaction of children with learning disabilities: a comparison of autism and Down's syndrome', *Journal of Child Psychiatry*, 36(6), 965–76.

Koegel, L. K. (2000) 'Interventions to facilitate communication in autism', *Journal of Autism and Developmental Disorders*, 30(5), 383–91.

Koegel, L. K. *et al.* (1997) 'Variables related to differences in standardised test outcomes for children with autism', *Journal of Autism and Developmental Disorders*, 27(3), 233–40.

Koegel, L. K. *et al.* (1999) 'Pivotal response intervention 1: overview of approach', *Journal of the Association of Persons with a Severe Handicap*, 24, 174–85.

Kugler, B. (1998) 'The differentiation between autism and Asperger syndrome', *Autism*, 2(1), 11–32.

LaVigna, G. W. and Donnellan, A. M. (1986) *Alternatives to punishment: solving behavior problems with non-aversive strategies.* New York: Irvington.

Lawson, W. (1998) *Life behind glass, a personal account of autistic spectrum disorder,* Lismore, Australia: Southern Cross University Press.

LeCouteur, A. *et al.* (1989) 'Autism diagnostic interview: a semi-structured interview for parents an caregivers of autistic persons', *Journal of Autism and Developmental Disorders*, 19, 363–87.

LeCouteur, A. *et al.* (1996) 'A broader phenotype of autism: the clinical spectrum in twins', *Journal of Child Psychology and Psychiatry*, 37, 785–801.

Leekam, S. *et al.* (2000) 'Comparison of ICD-10 and Gillberg's criteria for Asperger syndrome', *Autism*, 4(1), 11–28.

Leicestershire County Council and Fosse Health Trust (1998) *Autism: how to help your young child.* London: NAS.

Lewis, J. (1999) 'Using a digital camera as an aid to developing emotional understanding in children with autism', in Jones, G. (ed.) *Good Autism Practice September, 1999.* Birmingham: University of Birmingham.

Lister Brook, S. and Bowler, D. (1992) 'Autism by another name? Semantic and pragmatic impairments in children', *Journal of Autism and Developmental Disorders*, 22, 61–82.

Lord, C. (1985) 'Autism and comprehension of language', in Schopler, E. and Mesibov, G. B. (eds) *Communication problems in autism.* New York: Plenum Press.

Lord, C. (2000) 'Commentary: achievements and future directions for intervention research in communication and autism spectrum disorders', *Journal of Autism and Developmental Disorders*, 30(5), 393–8.

Lord, C. *et al.* (1989) 'Autistic diagnostic observation schedule: a standardised observation of communicative and social behaviour', *Journal of Autism and Developmental Disorders*, 20, 115–29.

Lord, C. *et al.* (1994) 'Autism Diagnostic Interview-Revised: a revised version of a diagnostic interview for carers of individuals with possible pervasive developmental disorders', *Journal of Autism and Developmental Disorders*, 24, 659–85.

Lord, C. *et al.* (2000) 'The Autism Diagnostic Observation Schedule- Generic: a standard measure of social and communication deficits associated with the spectrum of autism', *Journal of Autism and Developmental Disorders*, 30(3), 205.

Lord, C. and Schopler, E. (1987) 'Neurobiological implications of sex differences in autism', in Schopler, E. and Mesibov, G. (eds) *Neurobiological issues in autism.* New York: Plenum.

Lovaas, O. I. (1987) 'Behavioral treatment and normal intellectual and educational functioning in autistic children', *Journal of Consulting and Clinical Psychology*, 55, 3–9.

Lubbock, J. (2001) 'In the balance: the Lovaas experience', in Richer, J. and Coates, S. (eds) *Autism: in search of coherence*. London: Jessica Kingsley.

McCann, J. and Roberts, S. (1999) 'An holistic approach to communication at Wargrave House school', in Jones, G. (ed.) *Good Autism Practice, September 1999*. Birmingham: University of Birmingham.

McCarthy, M. (1999) *Sexuality and women with learning disabilities*. London: Jessica Kingsley.

McGregor, E. and Campbell, E. (2001) 'The attitudes of teachers in Scotland to the integration of children with autism into mainstream schools', *Autism*, 5(1), 189–207.

MacLeod, A. (1999) 'The Birmingham community support scheme for adults with Asperger syndrome', *Autism*, 3(2), 177–92.

Maddock, P. (1996) 'Sexuality: a framework for the development of policy procedures and guidelines in schools for children with autism', Confederation of Service Providers for People with Autism (COSPPA). Available from Wargrave House school, Wargrave Road, Newton-le-Willows, Merseyside, WA12 8RS.

Martin, N. (2002) 'Dyslexia and children with Asperger syndrome', *Good Autism Practice Journal*, 3(1), 58–62.

Medical Research Council (2001) *Review of autism research: epidemiology and causes*. London: MRC at www.mrc.ac.uk

Mental Health Foundation (2001) *All about autistic spectrum disorders: a booklet for parents and carers*. London: Mental Health Foundation. Costs £2–00 from the Foundation for Learning Disabilities, 20/21 Cornwall Terrace, London, NW1 4QL.

Mesibov, G. B. (1984) 'Social skills training with verbal autistic adolescents and adults: a program model', *Journal of Autism and Developmental Disorders*, 14(4), 395–403.

Mesibov, G. B. (1993) 'Treatment outcome is encouraging: comments on McEachin *et al.*', *American Journal of Mental Retardation*, 97, 379–80.

Mesibov, G. B. (1997) 'Formal and informal measures of the effectiveness of the TEACCH program'. *Autism: the International Journal of Research and Practice*, 1, 25–35.

Meyer, R. N. (2001) *Asperger syndrome employment workbook*, London: Jessica Kingsley.

Morgan, H. (ed.) (1996) *Adults with autism: a guide to theory and practice*. Cambridge: Cambridge University Press.

Morgan, H. *et al.* (1996) 'Developing a support model within a further education college for adults with autism', in Morgan, H. (ed.) *Adults with autism*. Cambridge: Cambridge University Press.

Moxon, L. and Gates, D. (2001) 'Children with autism: supporting the transition to adulthood', *Educational and Child Psychology*, 18(2), 28–40.

Mudford, O. *et al.* (2001) 'Parent-managed behavioral treatment for preschool children with autism: some characteristics of UK programs', *Research in Developmental Disabilities*, 22, 173–82.

Murray, D. (1997) 'Autism and information technology: therapy with computers', in Powell, S. and Jordan, R. (eds) *Autism and learning*. London: David Fulton Publishers.

Murray, D. (1999) 'Potions, pills and human rights', in Jones, G. (ed.) *Good Autism Practice, April 1999*. Birmingham: Birmingham University.

Myles B. S. *et al.* (2000a) *Asperger syndrome and sensory issues: practical solutions for making sense of the world*, KS: Autism Asperger Publishing Company.

Myles, B. S. *et al.* (2000b) *Asperger Syndrome Diagnostic Scale*. Austin, TX: Pro-Ed.

Nally, B. *et al.* (2000) 'The management of television and video by parents of children with autism', *Autism*, 4(3), 331–8.

National Autistic Society (1996) *Approaches to autism (Third edition)*. London: NAS.

National Autistic Society (2000) *Schools, units and classes*. London: NAS.

Neale, M. D. (1989) *The Neale analysis of reading ability* (revised British edition). Windsor: NFER-Nelson.

Newson, E. (1993) 'Play-based assessment in the special needs classroom', in Harris, J. (ed.) *Innovations in educating children with severe learning difficulties*. Chorley: Lisieux Hall.

Newson, E. (2000) 'Writing to children and young people with Asperger syndrome', *Good Autism Practice Journal*, 1(2), 17–27.

Newson, E. and MacLean, A. (1995) Social skills checklist. Available from the Early Years Centre, 272 Longdale Lane, Ravenshead, Nottinghamshire, NG15 9AH.

Nind, M. (1999) 'Intensive interaction and autism: a useful approach?' *British Journal of Special Education*, 26(2), 96–102.

Nind, M. and Hewett, D. (1994) *Access to communication*. London: David Fulton Pubishers.

Nye, A. (2000) *The autism handbook*. London: NAS.

O'Connell, B. (1999) 'The positive impact on the family on the development and understanding of a young child with Asperger syndrome', in G. Jones (ed.) *Good Autism Practice, September 1999*. Birmingham: University of Birmingham.

Olley, J. (1985) 'Social aspects of communication in children with autism', in Schopler, E. and Mesibov, G. B. (eds) *Communication problems in autism*. New York: Plenum.

Osterling, J. and Dawson, G. (1994) 'Early recognition of children with autism: a study of first birthday home videotapes', *Journal of Autism and Developmental Disorders*, 24(3), 247–57.

Ozonoff, S. (1995) 'Executive functions in autism', in Schopler, E. and Mesibov, G. (eds) *Learning and cognition in autism*. New York: Plenum Press.

Ozonoff, S. and Miller, J. N. (1995) 'Teaching theory of mind: a new approach to social skills training for individuals with autism', *Journal of Autism and Developmental Disorders*, 25, 415–33.

Parker, M. (2000) 'Setting up a secondary base for secondary-aged pupils with an asd within a mainstream secondary school', *Good Autism Practice Journal*, 1(2), 62–70.

Parks, S. L. (1983) 'The assessment of autistic children: a selective review of available instruments', *Journal of Autism and Developmental Disorders*, 13, 255–67.

Peeters, T. (2000) 'We educate persons with autism, but what can we learn from them?' Paper presented at Autism Europe Congress, Glasgow.

Perry, R. *et al.* (1995) 'Case study: deterioration, autism and recovery in two siblings', *Journal of American Academy of Child and Adolescent Psychiatry*, 34, 232–7.

Plevin, S. and Jones, G. (2000) 'Inclusion: a positive experience for all', *Good Autism Practice Journal*, 1(2), 8–16.

Potter, C. and Richardson, H. R. (1999) 'Facilitating classroom assistants professional reflection through the use of video workshops', *British Journal of Special Education*, 26(1), 34–6.

Potter, C. and Whitaker, C. A. (2000) *Enabling communication in children with autistic spectrum disorders*. London: Jessica Kingsley.

Preece, D. (2000) 'An investigation into parental satisfaction with a short-term care service for children with autistic spectrum disorders', *Good Autism Practice Journal*, 1(2), 42–56.

Prevezer, W. (2000) 'Musical interaction and children with autism', in S. Powell (Ed.) *Helping children with autism to learn*. London: David Fulton Publishers.

Prizant, B. M. (1983) 'Language acquisition and communicative behaviour in autism: toward an understanding of the "whole" of it', *Journal of Speech and Hearing Disorders*, 48, 296–307.

Prizant, B. M. and Rubin, S. A. (1999) 'Contemporary issues in interventions for autism spectrum disorders: a commentary', *Journal of the Association for Persons with a Severe Mental Handicap*, 24(3), 199–208.

Prizant, B. M. and Wetherby, A. M. (1993) 'Communication in preschool autistic children', in E. Schopler *et al.* (eds) *Preschool issues in autism*. New York: Plenum.

Quill, K. *et al.* (1989) 'Daily Life Therapy: a Japanese model for educating children with autism', *Journal of Autism and Developmental Disorders*, 19(4), 625–34.

Rapin, I. (1996) 'Developmental language disorders: a clinical update', *Journal of Child Psychology*, 37, 643–55.

Rocco, S. (1999) 'My comprehensive school: how I've enjoyed it so far', in Jones, G. (ed.) *Good Autism Practice, September, 1999*. Birmingham: University of Birmingham.

Rogers, S. J. (1996) 'Brief report: early intervention in autism', *Journal of Autism and Developmental Disorders*, 26, 243–6.

Rogers, S. J. (2000) 'Interventions that facilitate socialisation in children with autism', *Journal of Autism and Developmental Disorders*, 30(5), 399–409.

Rowe, C. (1999) 'Do social stories benefit children with autism in mainstream primary schools?' *British Journal of Special Education*, 26(1), 12–14.

Russell, J. (1997) (ed.) *Autism as an executive disorder*, Oxford: Oxford University Press.

Rutter, M. (1978) 'Diagnosis and definition of childhood autism', *Journal of Autism and Childhood Schizophrenia*, 8(2), 139–61.

Rutter, M. (1996) 'Autism research: prospects and priorities', *Journal of Autism and Developmental Disorders*, 26(2), 257–75.

Rutter, M. and Bartak, L. (1973) 'Special educational treatment of autistic children: a comparative study II: follow up findings and implications for services', *Journal of Child Psychology and Psychiatry*, 14, 241–70.

Rutter, M. *et al.* (1997) 'Genetic influences and autism', in Cohen, D. J. and Volkmar, F. R. (eds) *Handbook of autism and pervasive developmental disorders*. New York: Wiley.

Sainsbury, C. (2000) *Martian in the playground: understanding the schoolchild with Asperger's syndrome*. Bristol: Lucky Duck Publishing.

Schopler, E. (1998) *Asperger syndrome or high functioning autism*. New York: Plenum.

Schopler, E. and Mesibov, G. (1995) 'Structured teaching in the TEACCH approach', in

E. Schopler and G. Mesibov (eds) *Learning and cognition in autism*. New York: Plenum Press.

Schopler, E. *et al.* (1988) *The Childhood Autism Rating Scale*, Los Angeles, CA: Western Psychological Services.

Schreibman, L. (1988) *Autism*, Newbury Park: Sage.

Scott, F. *et al.* (2002) 'The CAST (Childhood Asperger Syndrome Test): preliminary development of a UK screen for primary-school-age children', *Autism*, **6**(1), 9–31.

Seach, D. (1998) *Autistic spectrum disorder: positive approaches for teaching children with asd*. Tamworth: NASEN.

Sebba, J. and Sachdev, D. (1997) *What works in inclusive education?* London: Barnardo's.

Shattock, P. and Savery, D. (1997) *Autism as a metabolic disorder*. Sunderland University: Autism Research Unit.

Sherratt, D. (1999) 'The importance of play', in Jones, G. (ed.) *Good Autism Practice, September, 1999*. Birmingham: University of Birmingham.

Sherratt, D. and Peter, M. (2002) *Developing play and drama in children with autistic spectrum disorders*. London: David Fulton Publishers.

Shields, J. (2001) 'The NAS EarlyBird Programme: partnership with parents in early intervention', *Autism*, **5**(1), 49–56.

Smith C. (2001) 'Social stories', *Good Autism Practice Journal*, **2**(1), 16–25.

Snyder-McLean, L. *et al.* (1984) 'Structuring joint attention routines: a strategy for facilitating communication and language development in the classroom', *Seminars in speech and language*, New York.

Sparrow, S. S. *et al.* (1984) *Vineland Adaptive Behavior Scales*. Circle Pines: American Guidance Service.

Spence, G. and Penney, J. (1991) 'Practical strategies in the workplace', in Nye, A. (ed.) *The autism handbook*, London: NAS.

Sussman, F. (1999) *More than words*. Ontario: Hanen Centre.

Taylor, G. (1997) 'Community building in schools: developing a circle of friends', *Educational and child psychology*, **14**, 45–50.

Tew, T. (1999) 'Sexuality and adults with autism: issues and strategies', in Jones, G. (ed.) *Good Autism Practice, April 1999*. Birmingham: University of Birmingham.

Thorndike, R. L. *et al.* (1986) *The Stanford Binet intelligence scale (Fourth edition)* Chicago: Riverside.

Tissot, C. *et al.* (2001) 'Addressing system failures for children with autism', *Educational and Child Psychology*, **18**(2), 63–75.

Van Bourgondien, M. *et al.* (1997) 'Sexual behavior in adults with autism', *Journal of Autism and Developmental Disorders*, **27**(2).

Venter, A. *et al.* (1992) 'A follow-up study of high-functioning autistic children', *Journal of Child Psychology and Psychiatry and Allied Disciplines*, **33**, 489–507.

Volkmar, F. R. and Lord, C. (1998) 'Diagnosis and definition of autism and other pervasive developmental disorders', in Volkmar, F. R. (ed.) *Autism and pervasive developmental disorders*. Cambridge: Cambridge University Press.

Volkmar, F. R. and Nelson, D. S. (1990) 'Seizure disorders in autism', *Journal of American Academic Child and Adolescent Psychiatry*, **29**, 127–9.

Walker, M. (1980) *The Makaton Vocabulary (revised)*. Camberley: The Makaton Vocabulary Development Project.

Waring, R. H. and Klovrza, L. V. (2000) 'Sulphur metabolism in autism', *Journal of Nutritional and Environmental Medicine*, 10, 25–32.

Watters, R. G. and Watters, W. E. (1980) 'Decreasing self-stimulatory behavior with physical exercise in a group of autistic boys', *Journal of Autism and Developmental Disorders*, 10, 379–87.

Webb, T. (1999) 'Look who's talking', *Special Children*, April/May, 31–3.

Webb, T. (2000) 'Can children with autism be taught to communicate using PECS?' *Good Autism Practice Journal*, 1(1), 29–42.

Wechsler, D. (1992) *Wechsler Intelligence Scale for Children – Third UK edition*. London: The Psychological Corporation.

Weiss, B. (1998) 'Routine monitoring of the effectiveness of child psychotherapy', *Journal of Child Psychology and Psychiatry*, 39, 943–50.

West Midlands SEN Regional Partnership (2001) *Report on autistic spectrum disorders*. Warwick: Warwickshire LEA.

Wetherby, A. M. and Prutting, C. A. (1984) 'Profiles of communicative and cognitive social abilities in autistic children', *Journal of Speech and Hearing Research*, 27, 364–77.

Whitaker, P. (2001) *Challenging behaviour and autism*. London: NAS.

Whitaker, P. *et al.* (1998) 'Children with autism and peer group support: using circles of friends', *British Journal of Special Education*, 25(2), 60–4.

White, C. M. (2001) 'The Social Play Record: the development and evaluation of a new instrument for assessing and guiding the social play of children with autistic spectrum disorders', Unpublished MEd thesis: University of Birmingham.

Whitely, P. and Shattock, P. (1997) *Guidelines for the implementation of a gluten and/or casein free diet with people with autism and associated disorders*. Sunderland: Autism Research Unit, Sunderland University.

Whitely, P. *et al.* (1999) 'A gluten-free diet as an intervention for autism and associated spectrum disorders: preliminary findings', *Autism*, 3(1), 45–65.

Wiggs, L. and Stores, G. (1996) 'Severe sleep disturbance and daytime challenging behaviour in children with severe learning disabilities', *Developmental Medicine and Child Neurology*, 41(8), 568–73.

Wilkner Svanfeldt, P. *et al.* (2000) 'They tell me I have Asperger syndrome, what is that? A way of giving information about Asperger syndrome to young people diagnosed as Asperger syndrome'. Paper presented at the Autism Europe Conference, Glasgow, May 2000.

Williams, D. (1996) *Autism: an inside-out approach*. London: Jessica Kingsley.

Wimpory, D. *et al.* (1995) 'Musical interaction therapy for children with autism: an illustrative case study with a 2 year follow up'. Brief report. *Journal of Autism and Developmental Disorders*, 25, 541–52.

Wing, L. (1981) 'Sex ratios in early childhood autism and related conditions', *Psychiatry Research*, 5, 129–37.

Wing, L. (1988) 'The continuum of autistic characteristics', in Schopler, E. and Mesibov, G. (eds) *Diagnosis and assessment in autism*. New York: Plenum Press.

Wing, L. (1996a) *The autistic spectrum*. London: Constable.

Wing, L. (1996b) 'Autistic spectrum disorders: no evidence for or against an increase in prevalence', *British Medical Journal*, **312**, 327–8.

Wing, L. (2001) 'The epidemiology of autistic spectrum disorders: is the prevalence rising?' *Mental Retardation Developmental Disabilities Review.*

Wing, L. and Gould, J. (1979) 'Severe impairments of social interaction and associated abnormalities in children: epidemiology and classification', *Journal of Autism and Developmental Disorders*, **9**, 11–29.

Wing, L. *et al.* (2002) 'The diagnostic interview for social and communication disorders: background, inter-rater reliability and clinical use', *Journal of Child Psychology and Psychiatry*, **43**, 307–25.

World Health Organisation (1992) *International Statistical Classification of Diseases and Related Health Problems*, Tenth edition (ICD 10). Geneva: World Health Organisation.

Zihni, F. and Zihni, F. (1996) 'The use of video techniques to develop language skills in autistic children', in Shattock, P. and Linfoot, G. (eds) *Autism on the agenda*. London: NAS.

Useful websites

www.autism-uk.ed.ac.uk	
www.autistics.org.	A site created by people with autism.
www.goodautismpractice.com	*Good Autism Practice Journal* This journal is published by BILD and contains articles on good practice in ASDs in relation to both children and adults. Articles are written by parents, by professionals in health, education and social services and by individuals with an ASD themselves. For subscription details, you can write to Marie Davies, BILD, Campion House, Green Street, Kidderminster, DY10 1JL or e-mail her on: marie.davies@bild.org.uk
www.hanen.org	HANEN
www.hivsa.ioe.ac.uk	EPPI Centre for reviewing evidence in education.
www.lookingupautism.org	A good site for resources on autism
www.lovaas.com	LOVAAS
www.musashino-higashi.org/english.htm	Daily Life Therapy
www.nas.org.uk	NAS
www.nas.org.uk/nas/earlybi/html	EARLYBIRD
www.option.com	OPTION
www.osiris.sunderland.ac.uk/autism	Autism Research Unit
www.pecs.org.uk	PECS
www.teacch.com	TEACCH
www.thegraycenter.org	Social stories

Index